# House MD: House MD Season Two Unofficial Guide: The Unofficial Guide to House MD Season 2

## By Kristina Benson

House MD: House MD Season Two Unofficial Guide: The Unofficial Guide to House MD Season 2

ISBN: 978-1-60332-065-8

Edited By: Brooke Winger



Printed in the United States of America

# Table of Contents

# Episode Guide

# Acceptance

This is the first episode of the second season of House, MD

## Synopsis

Clarence (LL Cool J), an inmate on death row, starts hallucinating about the lives he ruined and ended -- his girlfriend, a rival gang member and a cop. Clarence, in the throes of these images, screams to be let out of the room and then collapses.

House, finding Clarence's symptoms fascinating, barges into Cuddy's office and demands to be given Clarence's case. In particular, he finds it fascinating that the patient's heart was beating so rapidly that it began pumping air in addition to blood. Cuddy reluctantly gives him the case and House goes to the prison to visit his new patient.

Dr. Cameron meanwhile, takes on the case of a patient named Cindy who needs health clearance for her new job. Cindy appears to be a little anemic, and is at the hospital for further testing. The X-ray gives a clear indication of what ails her, however, given what she must have, it is odd that only suffers from a slight cough.

House diagnoses Clarence as hypoxic, with fluid in his lungs, and warns the prison staff that he will die in an hour without a respirator. House calls an ambulance. The warden insists that no death row inmate leave through the front doors. House has Stacy acquire a legal injunction, however, to get around this rule.

Cameron presents Cindy's file to House, who immediately diagnoses it as metastatic squamous cell lung cancer. The patient may have only six months to live and in his typically cavalier manner, House tells her to inform Cindy that she is dying. Cameron takes the high moral ground and is upset that House will treat a death row patient before he'll treat Cindy. Foreman too finds House's choice lacking sound moral foundation, opining that thinks heroin might be the cause of Clarence's tachycardia and pulmonary edema. House orders a drug test.

House's team examines Clarence, but he awakes and becomes agitated during the examination. The results come back clean—Clarence, an inmate in the high security hallways of death row, had managed to stay clean. As the doctors try to figure out causes and symptoms for the heart troubles, Stacy glares at House from the hallway. House shuts the blinds to his office to insulate himself from her stink eye, and requests an arterial blood gas test. After the meeting, Stacy, possibly forgetting every encounter she's ever had with him, corners House and demands to know if she can trust him.

Foreman draws blood from Clarence's femoral artery for a new round of testing. The tests results indicate a new symptom -- anion gap acidosis, raising the possibility that Clarence was taking non-conventional drugs in prison. The team mulls over the causes of anion gap acidosis, and Cameron throws out INH, the drug for tuberculosis. House sends Chase to the prison to see if Clarence has a stash of illicit substances.

Meanwhile, House has gone ahead and made himself comfortable, watching TV in the room of a coma patient. Suddenly, House's boob tube watching is interrupted when he gets a page that Clarence is dying. He injects him with atropine and calls Chase to see if he found anything, but Chase has only found boxes with office supplies in Clarence's cell.

House visits Clarence and pours him a shot of 150-proof rum, rationalizing that a dying man deserves a drink. He asks Clarence why he tried to kill himself by ingesting copier fluid and Clarence admits that he wanted to take control of his final days. House tells Clarence that the copier fluid contains methanol, which is poisonous, but the rum they just drank contains so much ethanol that it's going to bind with the formic acid and render it neutral.

Cameron stakes out a small area on the white board in House's office for Cindy's symptoms and House almost immediately erases it to change the topic back to Clarence. Why would he try to kill himself after filing for an appeal and how can they explain the odd accelerated heartbeat in the wake of copier fluid ingestion? House orders a full battery of tests even though Clarence's CT scan is normal.

House later returns to his office to find Cameron sitting in his chair. She has come to request a procedure for Cindy. House disagrees with her approach and says a biopsy would give more answers. Cameron protests and he ultimately agrees that if she covers two of his clinic hours, Cameron can run her test on Cindy. Cameron inserts a bronchoscope into Cindy's nose and she reports to Wilson that it showed no sign of infection. He tells her that she'll have to biopsy.

Clarence, meanwhile, is worsening, and complains of excruciating stomach pain, but Cuddy doesn't believe him. House, then, pulls back Clarence's sheets, revealing a large pool of blood.

The surgeons remove almost a foot of necrotic bowel from Clarence, and House muses about why Clarence killed the people he did. Popular opinion had it that Clarence killed his cheating girlfriend because of jealousy, his first cellmate for revenge, and an abusive guard for retribution. There is, however, no discernable motive for the killing of his second cellmate. House needles Clarence about it until he opens up: he felt like the guy could stare straight through him. Clarence, then, in a state of extreme hysteria and agitation, killed him.

Chase suggests that Clarence's rage was a product of adrenaline, but House theorizes that the underlying cause could be pheochromocytoma.

Wilson tells Cameron that Cindy's biopsy is positive and she is terminal. Cameron says that she just spending time with Cindy because she has nobody else—she is an only child and an orphan. Wilson admonishes Cameron to be more protective of her own mental health, suggesting that she could get some serious baggage if she takes it upon herself to be there for every dying patient that comes her way. Cameron, however, says she thinks that when a good person dies, somebody should notice and get upset.

House tells Clarence that he will need an MRI to confirm their nascent diagnosis. However, Clarence has prison tattoos, which are usually made with heavy metal that can cause complications and compromise clarity with the MRI. The MRI, however, still shows the pheochromocytoma. After the treatment, Clarence is pronounced cured.

Foreman talks with House about Clarence's tumor. Since it explained the rage attacks, it possibly explains Clarence's murders. Foreman plans to testify at Clarence's appeal hearing. House, however, disagrees that this tumor exonerates Clarence from responsibility. He says that a small tumor doesn't absolve Clarence of what he did. Plenty of other people managed pheo rage attacks on their own.

Cameron, meanwhile, hugs Cindy as she gives her the final diagnosis of her deadly cancer.

## Words of the Day

Pheochromocytoma: A tumor that secretes excessive amounts of catecholamines, usually adrenaline and noradrenaline.

Squamous cell carcinoma: a form of cancer that may occur in many different organs, including the skin, mouth, esophagus, prostate, lungs, and cervix. It is a malignant tumor that shows differentiation on a cellular level. Squamous cell carcinoma is sometimes developed in various mucous membranes of the body. This type of cancer is characterized by red, scaly skin that becomes an open sore.

## Memorable Quotes

Dr. Cuddy: (to House) Oh, so everybody lies except a convicted murderer.

Dr. Cuddy: What is it, Clarence?
Clarence: My gut!
Dr. Cuddy: Would you describe it as a shooting pain? A throbbing pain? Or maybe an imaginary pain because you don't want to go back to prison?

House: Do I have to spell it out for you? Pheochromocytoma. Actually, I'm not sure how you spell it.

Clarence: (about Cameron) That's the finest piece I've seen in ten years.
House: I could've hit that.
Clarence: And you didn't?
House: Eh.
Clarence: Then you're the one that should be locked up.

Clarence: Man, are you drunk!
House: Yes I am.

Dr. Cameron: (about her husband) I met him just after he was diagnosed with terminal brain cancer. If I hadn't married him... he was alone. When a good person dies, there should be an impact on the world. Somebody should notice. Somebody should be upset.

Stacy: If you didn't want me working here, why didn't you just say so?
House: I don't want you working right here. In my office. But anywhere else in the building is fine. It's a really big hospital.

House: She's got metastatic squamous cell lung cancer, six months, tops.
Dr. Cameron: Have you even looked at the x-ray?
House: No, just guessing. It's a new game. If it's wrong, she gets a stuffed bear.
Dr. Cameron: A spot on an x-ray doesn't necessarily mean that she's terminal.
House: I love children. So filled with hope.

House: Somebody left this (file) on my chair. Clever - forces me to either deal with the file or never sit down again.

Dr. Cuddy: It was just a consult? Did you expect us to shut down an entire floor for this guy?
House: Did you do something to your hair?
Stacy: You said you cleared it with (Cuddy)...
House: Come on. You've known me how long and you still don't know when I'm joshin' ya?

Warden: Your patient shanked one inmate his first month here, broke another one's neck, nearly decapitated one of my guards...
House: Relax - I've got a great bedside manner.

Dr. Foreman: Aren't there better ways to spend our time?

House: Good question. What makes a person deserving? Is a man who cheats on his wife more deserving than a man who kills his wife?
Dr. Foreman: Uh... yeah. Actually, he is.
House: What about a child molester? Certainly not a good guy, but he didn't kill anybody. Maybe he can get antibiotics, but no MRIs. What about you? What medical care should you be denied for being a car thief? Tell you what: the three of you work out a list of what medical treatments a person loses based on the crime they committed. I'll review it when I get back.

Stacy: I met Mark at a fundraiser that happened to be held at a...
House: You met me at a strip club.
Stacy: You were the worst two dollars I ever spent.

James: You can't go in there.
House: Who are you, and why are you wearing a tie?
James: I'm Dr. Cuddy's new assistant. Can I tell her what it's regarding?
House: Yes. I would like to know why she gets a secretary and I don't.
James: I'm her assistant, not her secretary. I graduated from Rutgers.
House: Hmm. I didn't know they had a secretarial school. Well, I hope you took some classes in sexual harassment

law. Does the word "ka-ching" mean anything to you? I'm going in now.

Dr. Chase: I don't agree with the death penalty in principle. In practice, however, I'd rather watch a murderer die than really annoy my boss.

Dr. Cuddy: So, what---everyone lies, except convicted murderers?

House: Don't worry - Mommy and Daddy are fighting, but we love you all the same as before. Now go out and play - bring Daddy some smokes and an arterial blood gas.

House: Little busy right now. Getting my drink on.

House: I have to make him all better for the state to kill him. Is it me or does that seem ironic?

House: Fine, Chase it is.
Dr. Chase: What possible reason could you have for sending me, other than the fact that you want to make me completely miserable?

House: Figuring requires deductive reason – I'm figuring you're doing no figuring.

House: I know you like (Stacy), but there's a code – bros before hos.

Dr. Wilson: Do you know why people are nice to other people?
House: Oh – I know this one...

Dr. Wilson: The man's in a coma!
House: He doesn't mind – I asked.
Dr. Wilson: You're getting crumbs on him!

Clarence: My gut - it feels like it's getting stabbed!
House: Well, he would know.

Dr. Cameron: Black defendants are ten times more likely to get a death sentence then white.
Dr. Foreman: Doesn't mean we need to get rid of the death penalty – we just need to kill more white people.

Dr. Cameron: I took an oath to do no harm.
House: Well, it's not like you signed it or anything.

House: You know how people say you can't live without love. Well, oxygen is even more important.

House: Nolo? I don't want to say anything bad about another doctor, especially a useless drunk.

Dr. Cuddy: You're addicted to pain pills.

House: But not useless.

Dr. Cuddy: You don't have access to the hospital mainframe.

House: No, but "Partypants" does.

Dr. Cuddy: You stole my password?

House: Hardly counts as stealing. Pretty obvious choice.

Dr. Foreman: What, don't you have an opinon?

House: Everyone has an opinion.

## Autopsy

This is the second episode of the second season of House, MD.

## Synopsis

Andie, a 9-year old girl with cancer, is about to inject herself with cancer medication when she sees the bathroom shake, and her hand is cut as the mirror shatters.

Upon arriving at the hospital, House is cornered by Foreman and asked for help on Andie's case. Her current diagnosis: currently in remission with terminal alveolar rhabdomyosarcoma. She is also hallucinating but because the cancer is in remission, there is temptation to discard cancer as the cause.

Despite input from his staff to the contrary, House asks for a tox screen and an MRI, and though both are clean, House notices that Andie's oxygen saturation is off by one percent. The other doctors resist House's request to look into this as a possible cause because the sat rate is within the margin for error. House, however, orders a battery of respiratory and chest tests.

As Chase begins to administer another test to Andie the sick little girl mentions that she's never kissed a boy and probably never will. Andie asks him to kiss her, but he declines, fearing the possibility of being accused of child molestation. She begs him, and he relents and gives a very appropriate, tender kiss.

The next morning, House returns to the office. Chase reports that all of the new tests were also clean. Foreman throws out an off-the-wall suggestion – neurosyphillis, which would be possible if she had been molested, or, for some reason, had sexual contact even though she is only nine.

House discusses with Wilson that Andie's sat rate has dropped another point, which Wilson says suggests a tumor in her lung, but still does not explain hallucinations. House thinks there is a tumor in the heart despite the lack of evidence in the testing they have done. The only condition that they can think of by way of a diagnosis is tuberous sclerosis. But the chances of one girl having two unrelated cancers at once are slim to none. House is thinking about exploratory surgery, risky for immunocompromised little girl.

House calls his team into the doctors' lounge shower and plays an audio file of Andie's echocardiogram in the acoustically perfect setting, asking them to listen for an abnormality in the valves of her heart. Cameron picks up on an extra flap in the mitral valve. House has a surgeon look at Andie's mitral valve under Chase's observation.

Chase pages House during Andie's surgery to report that there is a tumor that starts in the lung and extends to the girl's heart, running along the heart wall and thereby escaping notice by the MRI. Wilson informs the mother that the surgeons have to temporarily remove Andie's heart. Worse, there might not be enough heart tissue left to sustain her after the tumor is removed, and even worse than that, if the tumor has metastasized, she will soon die and there is nothing they can do.

During the surgery, Chase notices an abnormality with Andie's right eye. The next day, House and Wilson review the results of the surgery and conclude that the cardiac tumor was benign and was not the cause of the hallucinations. They soon realize, however, that the heart tumor broke off a clot before they removed it. He asks for a brain angio to find the clot.

House knows there's a clot somewhere in Andie's head, but exploratory brain surgery is not an option. When Andie hears about this very serious possibility, she exhibits no perceptible emotional reaction, prompting House to wonder if the clot is causing hallucinations as well as interfering with her emotions. The fear center of the brain is in the amygdale, near the hippocampus, but it would be impossible to operate on this part of the brain and keep Andie alive at the same time.

House pitches Cuddy on the notion of inducing hypothermic cardiac arrest so that they can siphon off two liters of blood and perfuse the brain while Andie's in an MRI. Cuddy thinks he will need FDA approval since he is technically talking about killing her for two minutes and then bringing her back, but because the procedure isn't invasive, House disagrees. Eventually Cuddy agrees to let him do the surgery with the condition that he must inform Andie's family that the procedure is not likely to work.

Wilson explains the procedure. Although the mother is shocked and confused, she agrees. House visits Andie and lays out the situation, explaining that even if it does work, it may just buy her another year of sub-par health, injections, pain, and doctor appointments. Andie still wants to try it.

Once Andie has been cooled and is on bypass, they have sixty seconds to remove two to three liters of blood out of her body and get it back in. If her body is bumped just slightly, she will die. They run a test procedure on a cadaver but every time any one of them attempts to intubate, the cadaver's head moves slightly. After many failed attempts, they decide to bolt her head to the table.

The next day, Andie's body is cooled down to 21 degrees. The clock ticks until time runs out, but nobody has seen anything. Foreman sees something four millimeters lateral to the hippocampus, and though no one else sees it, Foreman swears up and down that he did. They immediately begin rewarming Andie.

Wilson lets House know that Andie is going home. According to the surgeon's report, the clot was nowhere near the amygdale, which means that her fear center was working perfectly. Her calmness at hearing the news that she might die was merely because she was brave, not because her fear center was injured.

As Andie is wheeled out of the hospital, a large contingent of doctors and nurses is there to send her off with applause. She approaches House, hugs him and smiles.

## Words of the day:

Blood clot: This is the final product of the blood coagulation step in hemostasis. A blood clot can be benign, and even helpful, so that a wound can stop bleeding, or a clot can prevent blood flow in crucial systems of the body.

## Memorable Quotes

House: I'm taking a sick day.
Dr. Cuddy: Take some Claritin.
House: Everyone's a doctor suddenly.
Dr. Cuddy: You're actually talking about killing her.
House: Just for a little while, I'll bring her right back.
Dr. Cuddy: Oh, well, in that case go ahead. Why are we even talking?
House: Idolizing is pathological with you people. You see things to admire where there's nothing.
Dr. Wilson: Yeah, well, we're evil.

House: Can I come with?
Dr. Wilson: To tell Andie she's going to die? That's very un-you.
House: Well, she's such a brave girl. I want to see how brave she is when you tell her she's going to die.

Dr. Wilson: Go to hell.

House: True. Cardiac tumor was benign.
Dr. Wilson: That's impossible.
House: Statistically.
Dr. Wilson: Oh shut up. If the tumor's benign that means it did not cause her hallucinations.
House: That's why I'm mentioning it.
Dr. Wilson: So the tumor is a coincidence.
House: This is bad--you're starting to state the obvious.

Dr. Foreman: That CT shows no meningial involvement.
House: True. Get a tox screen and MRI.
Dr. Foreman: We can do that if you want to ignore what we just discussed.
House: Sounds good.

Dr. Chase: If she's never kissed a boy, it's a fair bet she's never had sex.
House: Tell that to all the hookers who won't kiss me on the mouth.

House: Union rules. I can't check out this guy's seeping gonorrhea this close to lunch.
Dr. Wilson: What's your problem?

House: These cancer kids. Can't put them all on a pedestal. It's basic statistics. Some of them have got to be whiney little fraidy cats.
Dr. Wilson: You're unbelievable!
House: If there's not one yellow-belly in the whole group then being brave doesn't have any meaning.

House: (discussing Andie's heart surgery) Chase, I want you there. I don't like reading surgeon's reports. They're boring.
Dr. Chase: I'm not really sure I should be spending more time with her.
House: She'll be unconscious. You'll be safe.

Dr. Chase: She's had one hallucination. Why are we operating on her? Why are we risking her life?
House: Because Wilson thinks it would be nice to give the girl a year to say goodbye to her mommy. I guess maybe she stutters or something.

Dr. Foreman: (listening to Andie's echo-cardiogram) What are we trying to hear?
House: A tumor.
Dr. Chase: They tend to keep quiet on account of them not having any mouths.

Dr. Chase: (listening to Andie's list of treatments) If it were me, I'd just stay home and watch TV or something and not lie here under a microscope.
House: Don't worry. If anything happens to you, nobody's gonna lift a finger.

Dr. Wilson: And not that it matters, but if you fix whatever's going on in her head, you give her maybe another year. Long time for a nine-year-old.
House: No. It'll just fly by.

House: You did it, didn't you? You kissed her.
Dr. Chase: It...it wasn't sick. It was one kiss for a dying girl! One small...one small kiss before she dies. (Foreman and Cameron turn away shocked) Thank you.
House: That's exactly why you can't touch my markers!

House: I'm not going to kiss you, no matter what you say.
Andie: It's sunny outside. You should go for a walk.
House: Not much for the long walks in the park. Git.

Dr. Wilson: She enjoys life more than you do.
House: Right.
Dr. Wilson: She stole that kiss from Chase. What have you done lately?
House: I'm pacing myself. Unlike her, I have the luxury of time.

Dr. Wilson: She could outlive you.

House: (Andie) genuinely is a self-sacrificing saint, whose life will bring her nothing but pain, which she will stoically withstand, just so that her mom doesn't have to cry quite so soon. I am beside myself with joy.

Andie: Lot of people.
House: Big musical number, kiddo. Lot of people here to make you look good.
Andie: You're kinda freaking me out.
Dr. Chase: He gets that sometimes.

Dr. Cameron: Whoa, you're letting me touch the markers?
House: It's written down in my advanced health care directive. Should I be incapacitated in any way you run the board, then Foreman. Chase, you're just not ready yet.

Dr. Wilson Hayfever?
House: You must be a doctor at everything.

House: Differential diagnosis. On your marks, get set...
Dr. Foreman: Hallucinations could be caused by...
House: Whoa! Wait for it. And...go.

House: And you stay away the patient.
Dr. Cameron: What did I do?

House: You'll just get all warm and cuddly around the dying girl, and insinuate yourself, and end up in a custody battle.

House: What the hell is this?!?
Dr. Cameron: Black walnut and ginger.
House: It's nice.

House: I should have been out of here 20 minutes ago.
Nurse Brenda: You got here 20 minutes ago.

House: (to a botched circumcision patient) I'm going to get a plastic surgeon, and put the Twinkie back in the wrapper.

Brad: (talking about circumcision) I got a pair of box cutters.
House: Just like Abraham.

House: Cancer doesn't make you special. Molestation, on the other hand...
Dr. Wilson: (I'm) with a patient...
House: Is she dying?
Dr. Wilson: No.
House: Then she can wait.

House: The tumor is Afghanistan, the clot is Buffalo. (Everyone stares) Does that need more explanation?

Dr. Wilson: We can't do exploratory surgery on her brain!
House: Are you sure you're not a neurologist?

Dr. Foreman: We could bolt her to the table.
House: Gruesome and low-tech – kiss me, I love it.

Clinic Nurse: The patient in exam room 1 asked for a male doctor.
Dr. Cuddy: (to House) The balls are in your court.

House: Is it still illegal to perform an autopsy on a living person?
Dr. Cuddy: Are you high?
House: If it's Tuesday, I'm wasted.
Dr. Cuddy: It's Wednesday.

House: You're dying, and suddenly everybody loves you.
Dr. Wilson: You have a cane - nobody even likes you.
House: I'm not terminal - merely pathetic. You wouldn't believe the crap people let me get away with.

# Humpty Dumpty

This is the third episode of the second season of House, MD

## Synopsis

Alfredo, who is a construction worker at Dr. Cuddy's house, complains that his asthma is acting up. She asks him to finish the job before taking a break. She feels extremely guilty when Alfredo falls off the roof onto the concrete.

In the next scene, Alfredo is being taken to the hospital in an ambulance and Cuddy rides with him. Not only is he unable to breathe, two of the fingers on his right hand have turned a bright shade of purple. Once he arrives at the hospital and is given a more thorough examination, House suggests disseminated intravascular coagulopathy, and asks his team for a cervical MRI and treatment for DIC.

Alfredo demands to be released so he can go back to work but a third finger is turning purple, and his blood his not clotting properly. House points out that if the hand is dying, whatever is ailing it has moved up the arm and even further. Cuddy orders a stronger, unconventional medicine

-- human activated protein C. House points out that this treatment is only for severe sepsis. Though aware that the treatment is incredibly dangerous and could cause internal bleeding, strokes and more, Cuddy tells them to do it anyway.

House's caveats are given more weight when Alfredo screams because he can't move his arm. The protein C caused bleeding in Alfredo's brain. The treatment is ceased and Alfredo is rushed into neurosurgery, which Cuddy observes.

The surgery fixes the bleed but not the issue with his fingers. A chest x-ray shows lung infiltration. His fingers become darker and he has a fever. Cuddy wonders if all this was caused by the trauma of falling off her roof, but Foreman reminds Cuddy that Alfredo had asked to leave the job, and ergo may have pneumonia. House asks Cuddy to check Alfredo's house to look for possible causes, and on the sly, has Foreman and Chase illegally search Cuddy's house as well since Alfredo has been there for the past three weeks.

Cuddy and Cameron find a rat killed by a trap under Alfredo's dresser, and conclude that the scars on his hand are from rat bites. His symptoms could then be easily explained with  streptobacillus. Meanwhile, In Cuddy's bathroom, House notices a fuzzy, black aspergillus fungus on the pipes underneath the sink. Looking at an x-ray, Cuddy agrees that fungal pneumonia is more likely than strep.

Meanwhile, Alfredo's little brother tells Cameron that Alfredo hasn't peed since yesterday afternoon. Cameron is concerned, and she immediately tells House that the amphotericin might have destroyed Alfredo's kidneys, which prompts Alfredo's mother to start crying.

The group huddles in and concludes that cause is not aspergillus nor rat bite fever, and the patient tested negative for moraxella, nocradia and cryptococcus. House takes Alfredo's temperature and sees that the patient's right hand is starting to rot.

House wants to amputate the hand but Cuddy refuses. House comments that Cuddy's hesitation to amputate isn't medical thinking-it's emotional thinking. He begs for legal clearance. Cuddy relents, and tells Alfredo that it is necessary, and he tearfully agrees to the procedure.

During surgery, things get no better as the fingers on the other hand start to turn purple. House wonders about endocarditis, which is a condition where the heart is infected with little bacterial blossoms clinging to its valves.

It is possible that some of the bacteria traveled through the bloodstream to the right hand. They then try to figure out what infection causes pneumonia and culture-negative endocarditis.

It can't be psittacosis, because Alfredo doesn't have any pet parrots. House and Cuddy barge into Alfredo's room. House asks the mother, in perfect Spanish, where Alfredo usually works on Saturday night, and somehow gleans that Alfredo works the cockfights on Saturday night.

House then puts Alfredo on the psittacosis meds, and Cuddy tells Alfredo that he is going to be fine.

## Words of the Day

Psittacosis: A disease caused by bacterium called Chlamydophila psittaci and contracted from macaws, cockatiels and budgerigars, and also from pigeons, sparrows, ducks, hens, sea gulls and many other species of bird.

Endocarditis: Inflammations of the inner layer of the heat. It can either be infective or non-infective, depending on whether a microorganism is the source of the problem.

## Memorable Quotes

Dr. Cuddy: Maybe we were right to begin with: his problems are all caused by DIC precipitated by falling off of my roof.

Dr. Chase: DIC wouldn't cause a fever this high.
House: See? My lapdog agrees with me.

House: Pinkies are supposed to be pink, right? I mean, they're not called "gray-ies."
Dr. Cuddy: But the organ failure is going to kill him!
House: But the pinkie is weirder

Dr. Cuddy: It's pneumonia. He wanted to go home. I thought he was lying. I sent him back up there.
House: Well why didn't you just take out a gun and shoot him?

House: You're not happy unless things are just right. Which means two things. You're a good boss. And you'll never be happy.
Dr. Cuddy: You figure a perverted sense of guilt makes me a good boss?
House: Now would the world be a better place if people never felt guilty? Makes sex better. (points to Stacy with his

cane) Should have seen her in the last months of our relationship. Lot of guilt. Lot of screaming.

Dr. Cuddy: All this from falling off my roof...
House: Yeah, if only he'd fallen on his head. Then he wouldn't have any of these symptoms.

Dr. Chase: How did you know about that key?
House: Someone as insecure as Cuddy has to have 20 keys in a 15-foot radius.
Dr. Cuddy: He lose that hand, he loses his job. All of his jobs. He's not like us.
House: He can't work as a cripple?
Dr. Cuddy: He loses his home, his kid brother drops out...
House: American dream destroyed. Very sad, very emotional. Not one medical fact in the whole pathetic tale. You've lost perspective, Cuddy. You've stopped looking at this as a doctor. You're acting like someone who shoved somebody off their roof. You want to make things right? Too bad. Nothing's ever right.

Robert: Look. My heart's red, your heart's red. And it don't make no sense to give us different drugs.
House: You know, I have found a difference. Admittedly, it's a limited sample, but it's my experience in the last ninety seconds that all black people are morons. Sorry, African-Americans.

Robert: I'll see another doctor.

House: Fine. Fine. I'll give you the same medicine we give Republicans.

Robert: I'm not buying into no racist drug, okay?

House: It's racist because it helps black people more than white people? Well, on behalf of my peeps, let me say, thanks for dying on principle for us.

House: (to Cuddy) If I tried a scheme like this, you'd get that nasty wrinkly face and screech like a hyena. Very sexy, I admit.

Dr. Cuddy: Why didn't you say you speak Spanish?

House: Because she'd want to talk to me.

House: (about Cuddy) I'm happy to report we're so in sync we're wearing each other's underwear.

Dr. Cuddy: Are you being intentionally dense?

House: Huh?

House: Oh my God. She's got pictures of you in here. Just you and...it's like some kind of weird shrine.

Dr. Chase: You're kidding.

House: Yeah.

Dr. Foreman: I'm not breaking into my boss' house.

House: I'm your boss.

Dr. Chase: She's scarier then you are.

House: She's a woman.

Dr. Foreman: You really want to screw Whitey? Be one of the few black men to live long enough to collect social security. Take the medicine.

House: You see the world as it is, and you see the world as it could be. What you don't see is what everybody else sees. The giant gaping chasm in between.

Dr. Cuddy: House, I'm not naive. I realize...

House: If you did, you wouldn't have hired me.

Dr. Chase: You two are just too nasty to each other not to have been...nasty.

House: Hey, I can be a jerk to people I haven't slept with. I am that good.

(about Cuddy's bed)

House: This is where it all happens!

Dr. Cuddy: Thank you very much. This guy's been working for me for a long time...

House: Do I get bonus points if I act like I care?

# TB or not TB

This is the fourth episode of the second season of House, MD

## Synopsis

In Africa, Dr. Sebastian Charles heads up a humanitarian effort to deliver food and supplies. One man from the tribe asks him for help for his son, who fell and isn't breathing,. As it turns out, the boy's lungs have deteriorated from tuberculosis. Later Charles is talking to a pharmaceutical company, Stoia Tucker, during a board meeting, pleading with them for more supplies to aid in his humanitarian efforts. They seem unwilling to help, and in the middle of the meeting, Dr. Charles collapses, and is taken to the US for treatment.

House isn't impressed by Charles, and disagrees with him that he has TB. Charles, who seems to be heading up his own diagnostic team, impresses Cameron, and she seems interested. House et al huddle about what could be wrong, and Chase notices a possible heart condition: sick sinus syndrome.

House meets with a woman in the clinic and determines she's allergic to her dead mother's cat. Unfortunately, the woman doesn't want to take steroids.

Then he observes Foreman give Charles a stress test, which shows that he has an abnormal PR interval. They schedule him for a pacemaker. On the way to being prepped for surgery, he offers Cameron a job and asks her out to dinner. Before she is able to accept or decline his offer, he suffers an acute headache and vomits, collapsing on top of Cameron.

The new symptoms indicate that the team needs to revisit the initial diagnosis of sick sinus syndrome, and House sends Foreman to deal with his clinic duty, giving him his nametag so he can still get credit for the hours. He meets with a Cecilia Carter who thinks she has cancer, which Foreman appeases by doing a biopsy.

Over in Charles' room the team runs a MRI test and Cameron notices that the TB test patch she put on shows positive. Cuddy interrupts a chat between House and Wilson and asks how it could be that a Cecilia Carter is currently complaining of Dr. House's poor bedside manner at the clinic?

Charles refuses treatment and tests for anything else now that he thinks he has TB, depressed that the medicine for TB isn't available to his patients in Africa. After a little thought he makes somewhat of a political statement, refusing to take the medicine to highlight the medical shortages in Africa.

Dr. Charles calls a press conference and Cuddy goes with him. Annoyed by what House perceives as theatrics, House takes away his cell phone, and unplugs his TV so as to allow Charles to better understand what it's like to live in Africa. . Charles goes ahead with the conference while House watches the live broadcast. House notices some troubling symptoms and barges in to the conference. He arrives as Charles goes into cardiac arrest, and effectively revives him.

Charles lets them do tests but refuses to take the TB treatment at first, but then after bickering with House, Charles agrees to take the TB treatment while they run more tests. House concludes Dr. Charles is suffering from an extremely small tumor in the pancreas that reacts to stress. They inject calcium into the pancreas to test their theory: if the patient's blood sugar drops they know the tumor is there. After a second dose they get a reaction but the blood sugar doesn't drop low enough. As Charles seizes, it drops at the necessary rate to confirm the diagnosis and they revive Charles.

Later Cameron says that she changed her mind about going out with Dr. Charles. House, feeling that Cameron has something of a Florence Nightingale issue, claims that she lost interest just because she knows that Dr. Charles isn't going to die.

Then, still being harassed by Cuddy about Cecilia's complaints at the clinic, House approaches her without his nametag. He hits her foot with his cane and then pretends to be a helpless cripple and fakes an apology. Cecilia is impressed and leaves. Cameron says goodbye to Charles who is off to Africa, but not before he has another press conference.

## Words of the Day

Tuberculosis: This is a common and deadly infectious disease caused by the mycobacterium Mycobacterium tuberculosis or Mycobacterium bovis. Most commonly, it affects the lungs, but can also affect the bones, joints, and skin. Over one-third of the world's population now has the TB bacterium in their bodies. As TB is highly infectious and contagious, those who have it must wear masks and take other precautions that occasionally even include quarantine.

## Memorable Quotes

House: You're allergic. We can control it with antihistamine. One pill a day.
Mandy: Pills?
House: You don't like to swallow?

Sebastian: People die of TB because we let them, it's our choice.
House: People die of malaria because we let them. They die of dysentery...
Sebastian: Nah, TB's my disease.
House: You own a disease? Well, I'm sorry I missed the IPO on dengue fever.

House: Insulting a woman with breast cancer! That's a move best left to the pros. Frankly, you don't have the chops!
Dr. Foreman: I didn't insult her! I did the unnecessary biopsy, like she wanted! It was negative, like I knew it would be.
House: What did you do? Call em perky? You are years away from mad skills like that!

Dr. Charles: Two pallets of antibiotics for tuberculosis.
Villager: We've got six pallets worth of patients.
Dr. Charles: Stoia Tucker needs a math lesson.

House: You are not the same as them (African TB patients). Your life is not the same, and you're cheapening everything they're going through by pretending you are!
Sebastian: I am the same, I'm not special.
House: You can't demand to be treated like any Third World sick person, and call a press conference!

Dr. Cuddy You've outdone yourself.
House: I'll say - my salad is covering a free T-bone steak.

House: I saved his life. That means I get credit for every life he saves from here on out.

House: (to Cuddy) Let me ask you something - if this were another doctor that this patient were complaining about, let's say, I don't know, Foreman, you'd just dismiss this as the paranoid bitching of another paranoid bitch and file it under 'P' for...
Dr. Wilson: Paranoid?
House: Am not.

House: He's not even a real doctor, he's a human telethon.

Dr. Wilson: Is that your problem with him? You see hypocrites every day, why is this guy so special?
House: You think I have a hypocritical attitude to hypocrisy? The problem is there are 26 letters in the alphabet and he only uses two of them. He treats thousands of patients with one diagnosis. He knows the answer going in. It's cheating.
Dr. Wilson: So it's all because he's one of them useless specialists?
House: Oh, did I hurt the big time oncologist's itty bitty feelings? You're a big help to patients who actually have cancer. Other times you're just annoying.

Dr. Cameron: He asked me out.
Dr. Chase: I'm shocked. I'm shocked when patients don't ask you out.
Dr. Cameron: He also asked me to come to Africa.
Dr. Chase: Boy, he moves fast.

Dr. Foreman: You figure that anybody that gives a crap about people in Africa must be full of it?
House: Yes. There's an evolutionary imperative why we give a crap about our family and friends. And there's an evolutionary imperative why we don't give a crap about anybody else. If we loved all people indiscriminately, we couldn't function.

Dr. Foreman: Hmmm. So, the great humanitarian's as selfish as the rest of us.
House: Just not as honest about it.

Mandy: The top of my head's killing me.
House: Hmmm. We spent a week doing "top of head" in Anatomy. I know just where it is.

Dr. Wilson: He cures thousands of people every year, you cure, what? Thirty?
House: McDonald's makes a better hamburger than your mother because they make more?
Dr. Wilson: Oh, I see! So you hate him because the lives he saves aren't as good as the lives you save.
House: Yup, that's the reason. Nobel invented dynamite. I won't accept his blood money.

House: The nameless poor have a face, and it's a pompous white man.

Sebastian: There's people dying in Africa of a disease that we cured over...
House: Yeah, I know. I saw the concert. Seriously, let's say you sleep six hours, that means every night you kill 1,440 people. I guess you gotta get some sleep, but come on, if you'd stayed up another 10 minutes you could have saved 40 lives. Do you send notes to the families in the morning?

That's gonna take at least 10 minutes so that's another 40 dead, another 40 notes...why don't you go wrack yourself with guilt in your own room?

Dr. Cuddy: Dr. Sebastian Charles collapsed during a presentation at Stoia Tucker.
House: Really? Crushed under the weight of his own ego?

House: Did you ever notice how all self-sacrificing women in history - Mother Theresa, Joan of Arc...can't think of anyone others. They all die alone. The men on the other hand, get so much tang. It's crazy.
Dr. Wilson: It's an unfair world.

Dr. Cuddy: Wow. Is there nobody you admire?
House: Well, there was this girl I met in 'Nam who could blow out a candle without using her...

House: That is exactly why the patient shouldn't be in the room. If you can't tell a man that his cologne makes you want to puke, how are you going to tell him he's an idiot?
Dr. Cameron: He's not an idiot.
House: Sure, you say that now while he's in the room...

Dr. Chase: What about something metabolic?
House: Welcome to the good ship "Ass Kisser." Nice day for a sail – pucker up, me hearties!

House: Every minute that we refuse to love one another, another puppy cries another tear.
Dr. Wilson: You're just mad because he's closer to a Nobel prize then you.
House: But I've nailed more Swedish babes. It's a crazy crazy world.
Dr. Wilson: It's not just a trip to Stockholm, you know. It comes with a cash prize.
House: Seriously? No wonder everyone's going after that peace thing.

Mandi: Is there something else you can give me (for my cat)?
House: Well, you live by the river – I've got a bag.

House: Take the pills or I let you die, do an autopsy, call a press conference, and let the world know you didn't die of TB.
Dr. Charles: Why would you do that?
House: Because I'm just a mean son of a bitch.

(talking to a reporter on the phone)
House: In my opinion, Dr. Sebastian Charles is an idiot. Yeah, you can quote me. C-U-D-D-Y.

House: Judging by the scratches on your hands, I'm guessing...new cat.

Mandy: It was my mother's. She's dead.

House: You keep a dead cat?

# Daddy's Boy

This is the fifth episode of the second season of House, MD.

## Synopsis

A young, about-to-be Princeton graduate named Carnell is heading out to a party to celebrate the upcoming ceremony. Soon after his arrival, however, he feels something like an electrical shock radiating through his spine, convulses, and collapses.

Carnell is taken immediately to the clinic, and House has to take the case because he owes Wilson for a $5,000 loan. House's first suspicion is that the young man was a recreational drug user, but his drug test comes up clean. He eventually cops to having taken ecstasy, but there is no established link between ecstasy and convulsions. . House, after telling the staff he just purchased a motorcycle, invites himself to Wilson's house for dinner. This leads Wilson to admit that he and his wife are currently not speaking.

The staff, acting on House's suggestion, examines Carnell's mother's medical history, and check for a genetic component. This research accidentally digs up a skeleton from the family closet: Carnell doesn't know that his mother died in a car accident that she caused. He had been told that his mother was hit by a drunk driver, a story his father was fond of repeating in tandem with a mandate that his son stay away from alcohol. After hearing this disturbing news, Carnell begins suffering from sphincter paralysis.

Meanwhile, House has some lying to do to his own family, calling his parents and telling them that he will be unable to meet with them for dinner during their flight's layover. As for Carnell, Foreman suspects a molecular memory of an earlier virus along the spinal cord and House orders more tests. Carnell isn't happy with his father for lying but then reveals he went on a trip to Jamaica without his dad's knowledge. House concludes he was smoking marijuana but may have been exposed to a pesticide. Marijuana alone would not explain these symptoms.

Cuddy isn't happy with House's lack of evidence, and her disapproval increases when he goes into another set of convulsions, develops a fever, and gets an infection because of his low white blood cell count. They administer antibiotics and send Cameron on a fact-finding mission to locate the guys that had accompanied Carnell to Jamaica.

House meets with Cuddy and apologies for letting his duties at the clinic go, trying to get her to schedule him with more hours so he doesn't have to have dinner with his parents or Wilson. She refuses and is going to be there herself.

Cameron, meanwhile, meets with Carnell's friend Taddy and learns that he has the misfortune of suffering from a fungus on his groin, and Cameron takes a sample. Carnell starts bleeding internally and is given more antibiotics. Taddy is convinced by Cameron to get medical care. House, after asking questions about the family's livelihood, discovers Carnell worked at a scrap metal yard owned by his father. The father, furthermore reveals he gave Carnell a lead plum on a key chain, and. House sends Foreman and Chase to get it. His suspicion, which turns out to be correct, is that the plum is radioactive.

After confirming Carnell has a tumor in his spine, they determine that they need a bone marrow transplant. House's parents, undeterred by his attempts to get out of dinner, arrive and insist he meet with them for a sandwich in the cafeteria. During surgery Carnell's heart rate and blood pressure drop, and Cameron and Foreman look on as House chats with his parents.

More complications befall Carnell as the surgery continues, and Cameron tells House that there may be nothing they can do for Carnell. Carnell's father, upon hearing the news, meets with his son and they reconcile over their mutual lies. They part when Ken tells his son that everything is going to be fine.

Cameron talks with Wilson about House and the fact his dad thinks he's a disappointment. House gets on his motorcycle and heads off into the night.

## Words of the Day

Radiation poisoning**:** Radiation poisoning is a form of damage to organ tissue due to excessive exposure to radiation. The term is generally used to refer to acute problems caused by a large dosage of radiation in a short period. Radiation can also be used to cure cancer: cancer cells divide and grow at a rate that far exceeds human cells, and radiation can kill the cancer while leaving the patient's own cells intact.

## Memorable Quotes

Dr. Wilson: We're discussing your new patient.
House: Must be a boring discussion, considering that I haven't accepted a new patient.

House: You lie to your mother?
Dr. Cuddy: Only since I was twelve!

House: (hearing serious news about patient on phone) Check it again. I'll be right there.
Dr. Cuddy: What happened?
House: Apparently I can save money by switching to another long-distance carrier.

Dr. Cameron: (talking about House) Why does he hate seeing his parents? So his dad tells the truth, he can't handle that?
Dr. Wilson: He hates being a disappointment.
Dr. Cameron: He's a doctor, world-famous! How disappointed can they be?
Dr. Wilson: You know what I figure is worse than watching your son become crippled? Watching him be miserable.

House: You - intravenous broad spectrum antibiotics. You - get cervical, thoracic, and lumbar T2 weighted fast spin echo MRIs. And you - track down all the other Richie

Riches who went to Jamaica. See if any of them have the shocks, the trots, or the hots.
Dr. Foreman: You have no evidence to support a poisoning diagnosis.
House: Which is why it's going to be so cool when I turn out to be right.

Dr. Wilson: If you have the money then why did you need the loan?
House: I didn't. I just wanted to see if you'd give it to me. I've been borrowing increasing amounts ever since you lent me $40 a year ago. Ummm, a little experiment to see where you'd draw the line.
Dr. Wilson: You're...you're trying to objectively measure how much I value our friendship.
House: It's five grand – you got nothing to be ashamed of.

Dr. Wilson: Now, be a grown-up and either tell Mommy and Daddy you don't want to see them, or I'm picking you up at seven for dinner.
House: What do you mean? You just said...?
Dr. Wilson: I lied. I've been lying to you in increasing amounts ever since I told you that you looked good unshaved a year ago. It's a little experiment, you know, to see where you'd draw the line.

Dr. Wilson: Two-wheeled vehicles that travel 150 miles an hour don't really go well with crippled irresponsible drug addicts.
House: Actually, two-wheeled vehicles that go 180 miles an hour do not go well with healthy responsible architects who don't know how to separate breaking and turning. Good news is, it brings the price right down.

House: Good morning!
Dr. Foreman: It's almost noon.
House: Really? Must be why I'm so hungry. Who's up for lunch?

Dr. Cameron: Why would you need $5,000?
Dr. Chase: Bad night at poker or great night with a hooker.
House: Thank you for saving me the trouble of deflecting that personal question with a joke.
House: When I said I'd do anything for the money, I obviously didn't mean it.

Dr. Cameron: Who was that?
House: Angelina Jolie. I call her "Mom." Who thinks that's sexy?

Dr. Wilson: You used me to avoid seeing your parents.
House: What do you care?

Dr. Wilson: I don't - I just thought it might be interesting to find out why.
House: You could have just asked.
Dr. Wilson: You would have lied.
House: You would have believed me, which would have kept us both happy.

Dr. Cameron: You're not curious?
Dr. Chase: I'm curious about crocs, but I don't stick my head in their mouths.

House: Get me out of this and I'll tell you who started the rumor about you being a transsexual.
Dr. Cuddy: There is no such rumor.
House: There will be...unless you get me out of this dinner.

House: Mom, it's great to see you.
Blythe House: Oh, Greg, don't lie.

John House: Last I checked, you have two legs.
House: (holds up cane) Three, actually.

Dr. Cameron: What's with the jacket?
House: It keeps me warm and cool. How does it know?

Dr. Foreman: It's dinner. It's sixty minutes, most of which will be spent chewing. Unless they say something like, "Do you prefer the chardonnay or the merlot? And, oh, by the way, we kept Greg locked in the closet for 17 years," you're not going to learn anything interesting.

## Spin

This is the sixth episode of the second season of House, MD.

## Synopsis

At a race, pro bicyclist Jeff Forster collapses while riding, falling off his bike and causing a mini pileup. He is immediately rushed to the hospital.

At the hospital, Cuddy tries to get House to work on Jeff, thinking he'll be interested in treating a world-class athlete, but House seems un-thrilled, figuring Jeff's respiratory challenges were caused by enhancement drugs, specifically erythropoietin (EPO). House's suspicions are confirmed when Jeff admits in front of his agent/manager that he injects himself with transfusions of red blood cells, and has used other performance enhancing drugs in the past.

House's interest in piqued now that Jeff told him the truth. He suspects he has an air embolism as a result of his injections and orders a test.

House is having lunch with Wilson when Stacy, his ex, stops by with her husband Mark for group therapy. Meanwhile, Chase is extracting the air bubble from Jeff when he starts slobbering uncontrollably.

Chase worries that he might have hit a nerve and House calls for more tests before heading out to crash Mark's group therapy session. Cameron prepares for a muscle biopsy, doing her best to hide her disapproval of the fact that Jeff has duped his fans by using performance-enhancing drugs. In the group session, House is unable to stay through the entire meeting when the head doctor, Louise Harper, picks up on the tension between him and Mark and sends House to a different group.

Meanwhile, Jeff's tests are all coming back normal, leading House to suspect that he may have encephalitis. Jeff's manager, unhappy with the speed at which her star performer is being treated, makes a donation to the hospital in the hopes of garnering more expedient service. During another test, Jeff once again decides to share his feelings and admits he took advantage of one young fan. After his confession, he goes into respiratory arrest again, with his red blood count dropping.

House concludes that either Chase missed something, or Jeff has cancer, and orders more tests. While meeting with a clinic patient coming off smoking and suffering from diarrhea, Stacy, meanwhile, harasses House about crashing group therapy to toy with Mark in group therapy.

While Wilson runs tests for cancer, Jeff wonders aloud if he brought this on himself while his manager accuses the hospital of making errors. Cameron, meanwhile, is passing moral judgment on him for taking performance-enhancing drugs because it's "cheating." Later, in a display of moral relativism, Wilson admits that he cheated on his wives but always came clean with them.

The tests show that there's no cancer and that Chase didn't miss anything in the initial examinations or subsequent tests. Cuddy comes in with Stacy, angry that someone in the hospital leaked information about Jeff's condition. House confronts him, asking him to admit if he's taken a drug called EPO, and Jeff claims he hasn't used it for years. House opines that his manager Moira told the press that Jeff had cancer so that Jeff could improve his image like Lance Armstrong. Moira denies she slipped him EPO, and Jeff fires her.

Jeff starts to recover but soon after, the doctors detect a thymoma that causes PRCA and ultimately results in anemia. Transfusions and hyperbaria keep the symptoms down, so Jeff's been treating himself all this time, until he stopped the transfusions and hyperbaric treatments. This exonerates Moira.

House, still wresting with his unresolved love for Stacy, asks her if she hates him or loves him. She cops to both and says that she loves Mark.

Cameron, still irritated that Jeff got away with cheating, makes her own true confession, revealing that she fell in love with her husband's best friend Joe, but she didn't sleep with him. Later House cons a janitor into letting him into the group therapy room so he can sneak a peak at Stacy's psychiatric records.

## Words of the Day

Thymoma**:** A growth, either malignant or benign, of the thymus. The thymus is used for producing T Cells. It is a rare disease, best known for causing neuro muscular disorders.

Doping**:** the use of performance-enhancing drugs including as anabolic steroids, Some doping substances such as alcohol, nicotine, and caffeine are permitted in low doses.

## Memorable Quotes

House: Trouble in paradise, two o'clock
Dr. Wilson: Your two o'clock or my 2 o'clock?
House: (points) There.

Jeff: There's no way I'd touch EPO. Too many guys stroking out and dying.
House: Damn! Ten bucks for the tickets, six for the popcorn.
Jeff: I do straight blood doping.
Dr. Cuddy: Plot twist!
House: That's a very daring confession.
Manager: We've got confidentiality, right?
House: Assuming I'm more ethical than your client.

House: She (Stacy) can't handle working with me.
Dr. Cuddy: Oh right, yeah, she's still got a thing for you, making it impossible for her to deal, makes perfect sense. Except for the pronouns!

Dr. Foreman: Anyone who thinks they should pay a guy money because he can throw a ball really far or pedal really fast deserves to be ripped off.

House: The air is keeping him from breathing air. Let's go with that for the irony.

Dr. Foreman: So if you break an arbitrary rule, Cameron damns you to hell. But if you break a rule that has a reason, that's designed to protect people, Cameron develops a crazy crush on you.

Dr. Cameron: It could be ALS.
Dr. Foreman: He's too young for that.
Dr. Cameron: Some type of muscular dystrophy?
Dr. Foreman: He's too old for that.
House: So what would be just right, Goldilocks?

Moira: Jeff is in the Lucas wing. If Mr. Lucas showed up needing a lumbar puncture, would he have to wait until tomorrow?
Dr. Cuddy: Mr. Lucas is dead.
Moira: Good – then there's an opening.

House: How's your recovery going? Got around to the small muscles yet?
Mark Warner: It's not the size of the muscle – it's where you get to put it.
Stacy: My goodness, it's like watching Oscar Wilde and Noel Coward in the third grade.

Dr. Wilson: You really really need to get some.
House: I get some "some" all the time. I always need to borrow "some" money.

Dr. Wilson: Is there a light somewhere that goes on when I have food?
House: Green for food, orange for beverages, red for impure thoughts. That bulb burns out every two weeks.

Dr. Cameron: We don't make careers out of who can stay awake the longest.
Dr. Chase: Really? Ever been to...oh, I don't know, med school?
House: You know me, hostility makes me shrink up like a...I can't think of a non-sexual metaphor.

House: This is exactly why I created nurses...cleanup on aisle three!
House: Go forth and scan his neck.
Dr. Chase: His neck?
House: Or repeat everything I say in question form.

House: How am I supposed to practice medicine with a lawyer sitting on my shoulder?
Dr. Cuddy: Responsibly.
House: You know I can't do that!

House: What makes a guy start drooling? Chase, were you wearing your short shorts?

Dr. Chase: You were right.
House: Now there were three wasted words.
House: You know, our relationship was way better when we were sleeping together. Why did we stop doing that? Did you get married?
Stacy: Yes. Otherwise I'd be on you like red on rice.
House: Look, rice isn't...oh, I get it!

Stacy: We need to talk.
House: Oh god, are you pregnant? 'Cause I really want to finish high school.

# Hunting

Hunting is episode seven of the second season of House, MD.

## Synopsis

Wilson and House discuss House's theft of Stacy's treatment notes, and the fact that he learned intimate details about the couple, including that they aren't having sex. As they leave House's house, they run into a man named Kalvin Ryan, who has been begging House for treatment to the point of stalking him. House tells him that he has AIDS and doesn't need additional diagnosis but Kalvin claims that he has tested negative for AIDS, so that cannot possibly be the case. A small scuffle ensues as Kalvin gets pushy, and Kalvin collapses.

Cuddy insists House meets with Stacy in case Kalvin files a lawsuit. They choose to meet at Stacy's house , where they bicker and Stacy complains that they have a rat.

Eventually, House accepts Kalvin's case but is clearly not interested by it. This changes when he learns that Kalvin is showing all the signs of fighting AIDS but is still getting worse. House suspects that the energy Kalvin's immune system is using to fight the virus is actually making him sicker, and orders more tests. House then prepares to kill Stacy's rat with a bizarre plot to get her fired by doing so.

While Kalvin flirts with Chase, House and Stacy head up to Stacy's attic to find the rat and are interrupted when his staff calls him about his patient. House quickly advocates some tests and treatments but is more concerned with killing the rat.

Meanwhile, at the hospital, Kalvin's tox screen shows that he has been taking recreational drugs. He starts to cough and then hacks up blood onto Cameron's face.

Cameron is given an anti-viral treatment to fend off the virus, while House ponders the new symptom, a ruptured blood vessel in the lung. Cameron opines that Calvin's recreational drugs may be contaminated. While she and Chase disappear to conduct a search of Kalvin's apartment, House describes Stacey's rat's odd behavior to Foreman to get a diagnosis.

After gaining entry to Kalvin's apartment, they find Kalvin's photos of broken 1930 fluorescents that contained beryllium, a substance that can inflame the lungs and inhibit breathing. Kalvin is subjected to a lung biopsy and shares with Cameron, upon her return, that he brought some of his drugs to the hospital, in hopes of a positive reaction for some reason.

Back at Stacy's, House breaks in, determined to get to the bottom of her rat situation. He informs her that the rat has a tumor that might be caused by something in the house. He leaves after Mark calls, but not before engaging in passive aggressive behavior in hopes of annoying her.

Kalvin goes into respiratory distress and asks them to tell his father he's sorry, even though his father kicked him out of the house. Meanwhile, Foreman has a new diagnosis: he has a tumor on the heart. CT confirms his suspicion but Cameron believes it may be a non-lethal mass and House instructs her conduct the test to confirm. As Cameron conducts her test and reveals that she hid his drugs, Kalvin suggests that HIV might actually loosen her up since she no longer has to play by the rules.

House, still hell-bent on solving this rat issue, tells Stacy that the rat's urine shows signs that someone in the house is smoking. As it turns out, Stacy has been doing it secretly and started two weeks after House's surgery. They start to consider a kiss when the rat sets off the trap.

Chase goes to visit Cameron, and as she is high on Kalvin's drugs, she seduces him. The next day Cameron shows up for work as House arrives with his rat (nicknamed "Steve McQueen") and quickly figures out she was using drugs. They end up at Kalvin's room to find his father Michael by his bedside, having a heated argument. His father claims that Kalvin killed his mother.

This is somewhat true: Kalvin's mother died because she needed a kidney and he was the only donor, but had HIV. It soon becomes clear to everyone that Cameron and Chase slept together, and they struggle with what to do about their potential relationship Then the tests show that Kalvin has terminal cancer.

House, remembering seemingly asinine facts (Kalvin's dad was sweating and they're from Montana) cancels the biopsy and concludes Kalvin's illness is caused by parasites native to Montana that mainly affects foxes. They can stay in a host body for decades, causing cysts, and Michael may have cysts in his liver. Tempers flare after this hypothesis in confirmed: Michael stands by his assertion that Kalvin killed his mother and House, who feels differently, is forced to punch Michael in the stomach when he takes a swing at him.

Father and son go into surgery and have the cysts and parasites removed. Cameron accuses Kalvin of trying to self-destruct and take her with him. House meets with Stacy who gets him ice for his bruise, while he informs her that Mark has to know about her smoking, and lets other information slip that clearly indicates that he's read her file. He excuses his actions by asserting that she wants him around. She disagrees, and kicks him out.

Kalvin and Michael make amends, Stacy seeks comfort with Mark, and Chase notices that his lip was cut when he slept with Cameron. Cameron worriedly anticipates the day of her first HIV test, and House is alone with his new pet rat.

## Words of the day:

Cyst: a closed sac with a distinct membrane separating it from nearby tissue. Cysts can air, fluids, or semi-solid material. Once formed, the cyst will remain in the tissue permanently and can only be removed by surgery.

## Memorable Quotes

House: Two successful surgeries, two lives saved. I'm over my quota. Can I have next week off?
Dr. Cuddy: Two family members assaulted.
House: It was self-defense.
Dr. Cuddy: You baited him.
House: You're right. I was asking for it. The low-cut blouse, the do-me pumps.

Dr. Cuddy: Go see Stacy.
House: We gave him EPI. He's fine.
Dr. Cuddy: You need a lawyer. Go see Stacy. You hit a patient.
House: Four words, two mistakes. He's not a patient and I didn't hit him.
Dr. Cuddy: Of course you didn't. Go see Stacy.

Stacy: Okay, I blow my smoke into the vents so Mark doesn't know.
House: I always knew it.
Stacy: Bluffing!
House: You started two weeks after my surgery. Menthols, then lights after a month.
Stacy: Why didn't you say anything?
House: 'Cause it helped me monitor your misery level. One trip outside was a good day, upwards of six you were in hell.

House: Steve McQueen without hair? It's a blessing he died young.
Wilson: Sooo... now you've gotta drum up another excuse to be around the love of your life. Could hit another patient.
House: Naah. Don't like to repeat myself. People will say I'm formulaic.

House: I am not treating you.
Kalvin: Because you're a closet case?
Dr. Wilson: We're...not together.
House: He's so self-loathing.

Dr. Cameron: Why do you have a rat?
House: Jealous?

House: Meanwhile, (Stacy) can't stop thinking about...I can't read that – is she obsessed with a "gray horse," or me?
Dr. Wilson: It says she thinks you're an annoying jerk.
House: It's a pet name

Dr. Wilson: (to House) Now you've got the proof you need. Just take those personal psych records to Cuddy – that'll show her Stacy is out of control.

House: Now let go of my cane before it becomes your new boyfriend.
Kalvin: Honey, I will marry it if you take my case.
House: Congress says you can't.

Stacy: You don't treat him, he charges you with assault.
House: Just because he says I hit him doesn't make it true. Watch – I'm surrounded by naked cheerleaders. (nothing happens) See?
Mark: What's going on?
House: It's not what you think. I now it looks like we're cleaning dishes, but actually we're having sex.
Stacy: We're working.
Mark: Wow, wish I'd become a doctor. This place would be spotless.

Dr. Wilson: Trying to win Stacy back by killing an animal. Very caveman.

Dr. Cameron: I have fun.
Dr. Chase: She has some scheduled for February.

Dr. Foreman: Bad time? Where are you?
House: At your girlfriend's place. Ignore the moaning and squeaking.

House: Gotta go – it's killing time.

Kalvin: This is none of your business.
House: You should have thought of that before you stalked me. Now I'm interested.

Dr. Cameron: So you always use a condom?
Dr. Foreman: Uhhh, yeah.
House: Brother's on the down low... got to.
Dr. Foreman: I'm not ready for any Foreman juniors yet.
Dr. Cameron: You?
House: Working girls - they're sticklers. You're not going to poll Chase?
Dr. Chase: I'm not an idiot.
House: Obviously not. Who doesn't sleep with a drugged-out colleague when they have a chance?

House: Okay.

Dr. Cuddy: That's it, "okay"? No name-calling, no squawking, no rending of garments.

House: I like this t-shirt.

## Mistakes

This is the ninth episode of the second season of House MD.

## Synopsis

Stacy is preparing for a disciplinary hearing with Chase and House, all the while firmly commenting that working with House is difficult for her. After a tense but brief meeting with House, she informs Chase that his career rests on a case, so he must review it and think carefully.

The patient, Kayla, sought help for persistent and acute stomach pains at the clinic. Foreman evaluated her symptoms and chose to run tests for nerve issues. House, at first disinterested, became interested when he realized that her iris was inflamed, and sends Chase to examine her for genital sores in retaliation for Chase spilling his Vicodin. He found ulcerations, later seeking treatment for a pustule on her arm. In Chase's recounting of the story, he tells Stacy that they didn't even go into an exam room, but relented and told the truth under pressure, confessing that he merely gave Kayla a stronger antacid and sent her on her way.

He called an hour later to follow up, and not long after, she was returned to urgent care due to massive stomach bleeding from a rupture. Chase cauterized the rupture but there was a perforation in her stomach tissue, causing the acidic contents to spread into the rest of her body and cause liver damage as well as sepsis.

During Chase's interview with Stacy, House is treating a patient that suffers from a persistent cough when Stacy asks him why Chase screwed up but House says he didn't screw up. He tells her that he spotted the second ulcer with the perforation, then chastised Chase because he didn't check Kayla for ulcers earlier.

After suffering the unfortunate consequences of her stomach perforation, Kayla found herself in need of a liver transplant, and suffering from convulsions. Kayla's brother volunteered to donate, hurriedly completing the necessary medical tests to prove himself eligible. House, meanwhile, bribed the transplant surgeon in order to get Kayla her liver as soon as possible. He also tried to blackmail the surgeon, Dr. Ayersman, to take on the case by threatening to reveal his extramarital affairs. After Ayersman performed the surgery, House told his wife about him anyway.

The surgery went well, but two months later Kayla returned and House forced Chase to examine her. He noticed a fever and ordered tests. Complications followed as her body began to reject the transplant. Kayla's brother, learning that his sister was rejecting the organ and possibly had an infection, rushed to the hospital. House at first wonders if the brother had hepatitis and faked the medical exam, but later concludes that he gave her liver cancer.

They operate on both of them, but due to the cancer Kayla rejected the liver and couldn't get authorization for another transplant.

After Kayla died a week after the transplant, Stacy stepped in to conduct an investigation into charges of gross negligence as Sam is pursuing the lawsuit against Chase. Stacy questions Chase further, and he admits that he told Sam that he was hung over and made a mistake.

House calls for a private conference with Chase and needles him about his admission of a hang over. He opines that Chase wasn't hung over but was upset—he had just received a call from his stepmother with the news that his father had died.

The committee then notes Chase did make a mistake and will get a one-week suspension, but they otherwise feel his father's death clears him of further punishment. They're not happy with House, however, and mandate that he is supervised by another doctor for a month. Cuddy selects Foreman to be the doctor that acts as his supervisor.

## Words of the Day

Ulcer: An open sore of the skin, eyes or mucous membrane. They can be caused by an abrasion and exacerbated by inflammation and infection, and/or medical conditions which impede healing. Other causes of skin ulcerations include pressure from various sources and lack of circulation.

Sepsis: A serious and potentially life-threatening medical condition, resulting from the immune response to a severe infection, oftentimes due to bacteria in the bloodstream.

## Memorable Quotes

Dr. Cuddy: Forget it. We can't give a liver to a woman this sick.
House: Do you listen to what you're saying?

Dr. Cuddy: Start praying for a 12-car pile-up on the turnpike 'cause we're not exactly swimming in livers over here.

House: Livers are important, Cuddy. You can't live without them, hence the name.
Dr. Cuddy: Dr. House, meet your new boss.
(everyone looks at Foreman)
Dr. Wilson: Guess I'm his best friend now.

Dr. Wilson: (to House) Your disdain for human interaction doesn't exculpate you - it inculpates you!

House: I've moved past threesomes, I am now into foursomes. If someone backs out then you still got a threesome, and if two people back out you're still having sex. You'd be amazed even if three people...

Stacy: Where's Chase?
House: He's too busy to service you until after work. I've got a few minutes, though. Feel free to say something like, 'What'll we do with the time left over?"

House: (opening his pills) Childproof? How many kids are hopped up on Vicodin?
House: Chase loves me...and isn't Turkish.

House: Oh, for the record, you're the worst transplant surgeon in the hospital...but you're the only one who's cheating on his wife.

Sam: Are you Dr. House?

House: Depends. Are you going to hit Dr. House?

Stacy: You have been hiding things and lying to me all day.

House: I didn't lie to you about anything...except the things I admitted to you I was lying about.

Stacy: If Chase screwed up so badly, why didn't you fire him?

House: He has great hair.

Stacy: What are you hiding?

House: I'm gay. Oh...that's not what you meant. It does explain a lot though. No girlfriend, always with Wilson, obsession with sneakers...

# Deception

This is the tenth episode of House MD season two.

## Synopsis

At a gambling joint, House and a young woman compare notes on the ponies when she convulses, and then collapses. House notices a series of bruises on her chest and sends her to the clinic.

This time, as per Cuddy's instructions, Foreman is running the meeting, which doesn't prevent House from scoffing at his diagnosis of a sexual or alcoholic-based disease. The diagnostic meeting takes a decidedly unprofessional tone as the two bicker in front of Cuddy, and she sides with Foreman with the caveat that he will have to take full responsibility for whatever happens. House runs Anica's medical history and asks her about Cushings. Anica says she had it a year ago, and had a tumor on her pituitary gland removed. There is, however, no evidence that she relapsed, so Foreman orders more tests. House, unconcerned about the lack of evidence, asserts she still has Cushings and Foreman relents despite his opinion she's suffering from alcoholic withdrawals.

Foreman finds out House has ordered MRIs for the entire maternity ward, and gathered a year's worth of discharge summaries that he has neglected to complete. Foreman, in his new role as supervisor, can sign all of the paperwork that has accumulated. Meanwhile, Cameron and Chase find a mass on Anica's pancreas and give her two months to live. Anica takes it well, and they prep her for a biopsy. Cameron breaks the news to Anica.. They take her into surgery for a biopsy with House assisting. Later House is called in to check out a woman with a vaginal infection resulting from using strawberry jelly as a spermicide.

Back in Anica's room, the biopsy proves negative and Cameron suspects she has Munchausen's, and injected herself with ACTH to bring on the symptoms for some reason. Foreman, in his new role as House's supervisor, sends House and Cameron to break into Anica's house. At the apartment they find she's visited several doctors but also has three pairs of eyeglasses, possibly indicating she has a tumor pressing on the optic nerve.

Cameron takes the consent form to Anica and accuses her of faking her symptoms and leaves a bottle of pills behind. The pills are marked "danger", although they are merely a pill normally used to treat UTIs. The pills turns one's tears and urine orange. Sure enough, she takes the bait and further tests are called off when it is revealed that her pee is orange. They decide she has Muchausen's.

While House goes through the files, Anica denies doing anything to herself to create or illicit symptoms. House then firmly opines that she suffers from Munchausen's and aplastic anemia. He suggests a bone marrow biopsy. Foreman is reluctant but eventually gives in. Later, Foreman approaches Wilson and asks if there's any way House will take him seriously as a boss. Later, House tells Foreman that the test was positive and Foreman calls him on his bluff, and bars House from Anica's room. Ultimately, Cuddy and Foreman discharge her without performing any more tests.

House intercepts Anica outside and offers to do the test outside on the bench while sympathizing with her history that led to her Munchausen's. He offers to give her a cocktail of insulin and □olchicines that will confirm his diagnosis: if she is faking, the injection will kill her. If not, she'll merely seize and be re-admitted.

Foreman's wondering why Anica collapsed just outside the hospital when Cameron confirms she has anemia. House gloats. Foreman goes to meet with Anica and tells her what her choices are: a risky bone marrow transplant or a lifetime of injections. She agrees to the transplant. They prep her: they have to kill the old bone marrow and then keep her in sterile conditions for two weeks until they can perform the transplant. A light suddenly goes on in House's head: she has an infection but her faked symptoms were suppressing the infection. House advises a safer course despite the low white cell count, and comes up with colchine, which he already has given her. He concludes that there is a bacteria inside her bruises that got into her organs.

Later, we see Anica at another hospital with her new symptoms, while at the gambling joint House places a major bet to win.

## Words of the Day:

Muchausen's Syndrome a disorder in which sufferers fake disease, illness, or psychological trauma in order to draw attention or sympathy to themselves. It is also sometimes known as Hospital addiction syndrome.

Aplastic Anemia: Aplastic anemia is a condition where bone marrow does not produce sufficient new cells to replenish blood cells.

## Memorable Quotes

Dr. Foreman: I don't see a regrowth, did you have the medical records faxed over?
House: Smart, not hard, that's my philosophy boss.
Dr. Foreman: I'll take that as a no..

Dr. Foreman: Yeah, you're all about the nurture.
House: Do you need a hug?

Dr. Foreman: You injected her against her will, just so you could be right?
House: She consented.
Dr. Foreman: She's mentally ill.
House: But she smells all so sweet.

Dr. Foreman: You ordered MRIs for the whole maternity wing?
House: I was in a crazy mood, good thing I got a new boss to back me up, although I think one of them was actually necessary.

Dr. Cameron: There's even books in the bathroom.
House: Either she's very smart or she has a fiber deficiency.
Dr. Cameron: Scan showed a mass in her pancreas.

Dr. Chase: Looks malignant, probably inoperable... I'd give her two months.
House: On the bright side, still means I was right.

Dr. Chase: Why don't you just get the sample yourself? Since when do you care what your boss said?
House: I don't care what anybody says, I care what they do. Right now, Blackpoleon Blackaparte has got the nurses on red alert, I can't get into the patient's room. So come on, I'll draw the enemy fire, you outflank them, get in there, get the bone marrow sample.

Dr. Wilson: (talking about House) And you want my advice on how to usurp him? It's very ancient Rome, you'll need a toga, of course, a sword...

Dr. Wilson: House assisting. That is funny. Too bad Foreman's gonna die.

House: Sorry, I missed that. Hearing's been off since the Ricky Martin concert. Some cholo kicked me in the head.

House: What else turns you on? Drugs? Casual sex? Rough sex? Casual rough sex? I'm a doctor, I need to know.

Dr. Foreman: She a regular at OTB. Somehow I don't see her holding down a nine-to-five and going to PTA meetings.
House: I was there and I have a nine-to-three job.

Dr. Cameron: It's the irony of women in charge, they don't like other women in charge. What, you think it's something else?
Dr. Chase: You sabotaged yourself. You went on a date with House, you slept with me. Putting you in charge of this department is like a sexual harassment suit waiting to happen.
Dr. Cameron: Yeah, they're really worried that I'm going to create a hostile work environment.
Dr. Chase: Maybe that's the problem. Being in charge means having to say no to House. Would you hire you for that?

Dr. Cameron: How would you describe my leadership skills?
House: Non-existent. Otherwise excellent.

Dr. Cameron: There's even books in the bathroom.
House: She's either very smart or has a severe fiber deficiency.

Dr. Cameron: She's got an appointment with her ophthalmologist on Tuesday and an appointment with her gynecologist on Thursday. Multiple appointments with multiple doctors...symptom of Munchausen's.
House: Or, just thinking outside the box here, she has a vagina and trouble reading.
Dr. Foreman: Dr. Wilson, can I talk to you about something in confidence?
Dr. Wilson: Of course.
Dr. Foreman: It's about House.
Dr. Wilson: Oh, then no.

House: Nice move, boss. Way to cover your ass.
Dr. Foreman: I just agreed with you.
House: Not because you think I'm right. You're just taking the safe route. You're a wuss. Don't worry; your secret is safe with me. Wilson!! Guess what Foreman did!

Dr. Foreman: What do you expect me to do, House? Quit? Cry?
House: Actually, I expect you to act like what you are--my employee, my subordinate, my bitch.

House: Do you like Teeny Tiny Moe in the fifth?
Anica: I went four for six yesterday. You want winners, cure me first.
House: Are you trying to cop a feel?

Do-Gooder: I took a CPR class.
House: That would be useful if she were having a heart attack instead of a seizure.
Anica: You might as well burn your money.
House: I'll burn my winnings – bigger flame.

Dr. Chase: Gambling doesn't take away (House's) pain.
House: It does when I win.

House: Chase killed that woman and Foreman's in charge?
Dr. Cuddy: Yeah, we have a pecking order here. If Cameron kills someone, Chase takes over. We have a flowchart in the lobby.

House: You probably shouldn't have sex for a while.
Hailey: For how long?
House: On an evolutionary basis, I'd recommend...forever.

House: At the end of 'The Boy Who Cried Wolf," the wolf really does come. And he eats the sheep, and the boy, and the parents.
Dr. Chase: The wolf doesn't eat the parents.
House: It does when I tell it.

Technician: You're going to need more blood.
House: The patient's empty.
Technician: Then I can't do it.

House: You can try.
Technician: I can try to look like Salma Hayek – that's not going to make it happen.
House: You may not have Selma's ass, but she doesn't have your eyes.
Technician: Yeah, right. How soon you need it?

Dr. Chase: I also realize that no matter what you do, you're still going to treat me like crap.
House: 'Crap' is a relative term.

# Failure to Communicate

This is the eleventh episode of the second season of House MD

## Synopsis

At a newspaper editor's retirement party, a reporter collapses and hits his head, babbling incoherently when he finally awakens.

At the hospital, House is conspicuously absent, off in Baltimore with Stacy to justify his Medicaid billings. Cuddy gives Foreman the reporter's case, and tells him to be especially diligent because the patient is Fletcher Stone, the famous writer. Foreman theorizes that Stone has aphasia because he is unable to draw or write anything. The diagnoses, however, is cast somewhat in doubt when a witness to the incident explains that Stone fell because his foot twitched.

Stacy and House are meeting with the Medicaid review officer, Peter Foster. House faces challenges in justifying his expenses and Stacy manages to intervene on his behalf and advocate for him successfully. After the meeting,

House observes that the cross she usually wears around her neck is absent, and makes mental note of it.

The staff administers a barrage of tests, and Stone's editor and wife, Greta and Elizabeth, are unimpressed with their diagnostic abilities. Fletcher has a respiratory attack and they're forced to intubate. Further complicating matters: test results show the presence of amphetamines even thought Fletched claimed he had given up drugs.

House, waiting at the airport for his flight, calls the hospital and goes over the aphasia case with Wilson, having gotten a heads up from Cuddy that the staff is having trouble. Fletcher is now running a fever. House tells them to get a medical history – Fletcher can answer yes or no questions even if intubated. The editor claims Fletcher is off of drugs but he takes sleeping pills, which Fletcher confirms but cautions the staff that he doesn't want his wife to know.

After administering a MRI, they find an old brain edema but Fletcher claims he's had no previous head trauma or symptoms. In addition, the edema is in a part of the brain that wouldn't necessarily cause the symptoms from which Fletcher suffered. The flights are stacking up in Baltimore, leaving House and Stacy together to make small talk as

House tosses out diagnoses of the various folks in the lounge.

Cuddy shows up to ask Foreman about his progress and he and Chase quickly duck out under the auspices of getting dinner. House continues badgering Stacy about her missing cross until she finally confesses that she and Mark had a fight, and is scared that he may want her out of his life. . Chase and Foreman have found anti convulsives in Flethcher's office desk. When snooping through the belongings of his wife, they find no other medicines. Foreman, meanwhile, starts getting nervous that he's on his own with this case, lacking House's expertise.

Meanwhile, Fletcher's condition is worsening, as he complains of stomach pains and a metallic taste in his mouth. Foreman is insisting on a lumbar puncture when House calls to advise them to put pressure on Fletcher to get him to be honest and leave out any details he may have considered uncomfortable or irrelevant. They confront Fletcher but he has nothing new to add. Cameron prepares to administer the lumbar puncture and starts to figure out what he's saying since he's still largely unintelligible. Meanwhile in Baltimore, the airport announces that all flights are grounded and Stacy shrugs it off, saying she already has a hotel room booked.

When they arrive at the hotel room, House needles her about her true intentions. They end up kissing but are interrupted by Foreman calling with the results of the lumbar puncture-he has an infection of some kind. House can't resist getting involved, much to Stacy's annoyance.

The staff goes over Fletcher's statements with House listening in, trying to draw patterns and figure out what he's saying. Cameron opines that Elizabeth's presence is screwing up Fletcher's speech patterns, and Cuddy lures her away under false pretences. Fletcher then makes enough sense for House to figure what's up and House concludes that Fletcher is bi-polar and has been drinking heavily during the depressive periods and taking weight loss medicine during the manic phases. House concludes that Fletcher underwent surgery that he kept secret from his wife. When Elizabeth hears this she is devastated. House recommends they test the blood by hand to confirm the diagnosis – cerebral malaria, which the computers missed.

Later, as Fletcher's editor tries to reassure him that Elizabeth will be back. Stacy boards her plane.

## Words of the Day

Aphasia: Aphasia is a loss or impairment of the ability to produce and/or speak or understand language, due to brain damage. Sometimes the sufferer can speak but not write, or vice versa.

Lumbar Puncture: Also known as a spinal tap, this is a diagnostic and at times therapeutic procedure used to collect cerebro-spinal fluid. The collection of the fluid can be with the goal to analyze it, or to relieve the spine of pressure.

## Memorable Quotes

House: So you had a fight. I'm sure it'll blow over.
Stacy It was about nothing.
House: Of course it was. Mark's tired. He's worried. He's got mobility problems. It's normal to blow up over little things.
Stacy: I don't mind fighting over little things. I didn't mind fighting over big things. That I could understand. We fight over nothing. You know, a mailbox with a sign that says, "Last pickup 5:00 p.m." Does that mean last pickup to go

to the post office, or last pickup to leave the post office and be sent out of town?
House: You fought over mail delivery?

Stacy: Why does this matter to you?
House: It's an anomaly. Anomalies bug me.
Stacy: Then you're going to suffer.

Dr. Chase: (to Foreman) The only thing you've been asked to do is supervise House in case he does something insane.
Dr. Cameron: Which might, you know, save a life.

Dr. Cameron: The more devoted, the more reason to lie.
House: That's cynical.
Dr. Cameron: You disagree?
House: No, I'm just kvelling. Our little girl is growing up.

Dr. Foreman: In one of (Fletch's) books he talked about giving up drugs and alcohol. Said how it changed his life.
Chase: Everybody lies.

Cuddy: You woke me up to lie to a patient?

House: You know, "Stacy" in the original Greek means "relationship killer."

House: (talking about Viagra) A woman has a heart condition, she's on her own. A man can't nail his office assistant, it's national crisis time.

Stacy: If I thought you were capable of listening, I'd shut up.
House: That makes no sense at all.

Dr. Chase: You're not my boss.
Dr. Foreman: I'm House's boss. House is your boss. The math is pretty simple.

Peter Foster: Are you trying to bribe me?
House: No. I could. There's an ATM in the lobby.
Stacy: My client is an idiot.

Dr. Chase: We've got an MRI scheduled in twenty minutes. Earliest Foreman could get the machine
House: I teach you to lie and cheat and steal, and as soon as my back is turned you wait in line?

Dr. Foreman: (to Chase) You have a point to make, or did you just feel like giving a long unnecessary speech for something medically irrelevant?

Dr. Wilson: Do you know your phone's dead? Do you ever recharge your batteries?

House: They recharge? I just keep buying new phones.

Dr. Cameron: Maybe House is wrong.
House: (pause) I hope that's not the end of the thought.

Dr. Cuddy: Tell me, if it is your aim to sell me the same crazy ideas that House does, how are you an improvement on House?
Dr. Foreman: I brought you a coffee!

## Need to Know

This is the twelfth episode of the second season of House, MD

## Synopsis

Margo Dalton is in the midst of getting ready for her daughter's birthday party when her arms spasms uncontrollably, and she backs the car into the garage.

House suspects Margo may be pregnant and gives her something to calm her down and allow them to do some basic tests. Meanwhile, Wilson confronts Stacy over her kiss with House and warns her not to lead him on. Stacy, in turn, admits that she's not sure what she wants from him.

Margo isn't pregnant, but she is undergoing fertility treatments. Foreman suspects she may have Huntington's, and when she gets irritable, he feels that her attitude is a confirmation of his opinion. He is trying to discuss this with the team when Margo has some sort of fit and they have to go into her room to see what the problem is, and calm her down.

House sends Foreman and Cameron on a search of her home to find evidence of any recreational drug use. They don't find any street drugs, but Cameron finds Margo's daughter Stella's Ritalin. If this is indeed the source of her spasms, the drug will be out of her system in twelve hours. When Foreman chooses not to release her until it's confirmed, House stops in to see Margo's family. He frightens her daughter with a poorly executed animal balloon, and interrogation techniques that are not quite age appropriate in order to see if she is on her Ritalin. Margo admits she never told her husband Ted and never gave them to Stella.

House then visits Stacy. She tells him she is leaving now that Mark has gotten better. House asks her not to leave, and tells her he thinks Stacy loves him more than she loves Mark. The conversation pauses in a long and uncomfortable silence.

Margo is discharged but in the lobby she has a stroke and collapses. House is called but he's not at the hospital; he's in Stacy's bed.

House eventually shows up and then collects on his bet with Foreman that Cameron wouldn't take her HIV test, and then tricks Cameron into giving him enough of a sample that he'll be able to conduct the test without her permission. They begin to work on diagnosing Margo's new symptoms and House suspects the Ritalin and the fertility meds conflicted and did something to her uterus, possible causing cancer. On the roof, Stacy meets with House and he wants to know if she is going to tell Mark, warning her that she's going to have to choose.

The tests on Margo come back negative and Foreman is unwilling to do a biopsy. Lucky for House and for the patient, Foreman's four-week-long position as House's boss is over. House reclaims his duties as presiding physician, ordering the biopsy for the suspected tumor. Before they can complete the biopsy, however, Margo starts bleeding from her liver—there seems to be a tumor there, not in her uterus. In an unexpected twist, Mark comes to House asking for advice, as he's concerned that Stacy feels like he is shutting her out. House refuses to help him and tries to go up a flight of stairs to avoid him. Mark tries to pull himself up the stairs and collapses from the effort.

Later, in a diagnostic session about Margo, House takes another look at her history. House opines that Margo was secretly using birth control pills during the fertility treatments, unwilling to tell her husband that she didn't want another child even though he did. The combination of Ritalin, birth control pills, and fertility treatments caused the tumor, which House believes is benign. Margo still claims she's not taking the pills but they do the surgery nonetheless. It turns out that there is indeed a benign tumor. The husband wonders why benign tumor was causing all those symptoms but the medical team eventually convinces him. Margo asks Foreman to lie and tell her husband that she can't take fertility treatments any more but Foreman refuses.

Cameron goes to House, who has her HIV test results. After delivering them to her, House confronts Stacy, who says she's going to tell Mark she's going to House. He tells her that Mark who is willing to do what it takes, not him, and he can't make her happy. He points out it won't end well and they'll end up back where they left it.

As the staff wonder how long Margo's marriage will last, Wilson sees Stacy packing up and he confronts House. Wilson, strangely emotionally invested in the potential relationship between Stacy and his boss, says that House sent Stacy away so he could keep feeling miserable, and so he won't have to change and lose what he thinks makes himself special. He then storms off.

## Words of the Day

Birth Control Pill: a combination of an estrogen (oestrogen) and a progestin (progestogen), taken by mouth to inhibit normal fertility in women of childbearing age.

Ritalin: An amphetamine-like prescription stimulant commonly used to treat Attention-deficit hyperactivity disorder (ADHD) in children and adults. It is also one of the primary drugs used to treat symptoms of traumatic brain injury and the symptoms of narcolepsy and chronic fatigue syndrome.

## Memorable Quotes

House: This better be important.
Dr. Cameron: You've gotta come back in.
House: No I don't.
Dr. Cameron: Margo's stable but...
House: Oh my God! I'll be right there!

House: We're done. Get rid of her.
Dr. Foreman: We're not done. We have to confirm the diagnosis before we send her home to die of something else.

House: Oh yes, the power tastes so sweet. You just can't resist, you're like a diabetic at the ice cream counter, you want to say no, but you need that chocolately goodness.
Dr. Foreman: Well, I'm still signing the charts. So until tomorrow you're not allowed to kill anyone.
House: Wuss!

House: She's not going to leave Mark in the middle of his rehab. Too much guilt.
Dr. Wilson: She left you.
House: Harsh 'tude, dude.

House: Peeing on a stick is only 99% accurate. Get a real pregnancy test. You know, the one with the blood and the hormones and the rabbit. (Foreman looks put off) Oh, I'm sorry. It's still your limo. What do you say, Miss Daisy?
Dr. Foreman: Whatever you want.
House: Lame duck's done quacking.
Dr. Foreman: You quack, people shoot at you. Cuddy just put me here to make you miserable. Another two days, you can go back to making yourself miserable.

(finding Ritalin)
House: Cocaine with a PG rating.

House: Ultrasound her uterus this time. See if there's something growing in there that doesn't look adorable in a onesie. (edit)

Dr. Cuddy: He's actually on time.
Dr. Wilson: He's six minutes early.
Dr. Cuddy: Something's happened.
Dr. Wilson: I'm on it.

House: Wow. It's a big jump from "Infidelity is morally wrong" to "Do her."

House: What does the flailing look like?
Dr. Chase: Her arms spasm uncontrollably and there's a mild facial twitch.
House: Demonstration?
Dr. Foreman: (impatiently) You wanna know what it looks like, go see the patient.
House: Ooo, snarky. Was he like this the whole time I was gone?

House: (to the whiteboard) We give you so much, and you give us so little.

Dr. Cuddy: Here's what I think she's gonna say: "Oh I love Greg, but if you go against a patient's wishes, you're calling her a liar. And if something goes wrong, I end up in court having to defend the big, mean doctor, albeit with dreamy eyes, who wouldn't believe the nice suburban mom. And even though his cane makes me melt, do the damn surgery."

House: Foreman, need your help here. You want to pull a bank job, would you go it alone? You gonna rob a house, sure, it's a one- or two-man crew. A bank...a lookout, getaway driver...
Dr. Foreman: I'm not saying anything till this metaphor plays itself out.

House: Cameron... I love you. Get your test results tomorrow.

House: Who finished the animal crackers? If you finish something, don't just put back the empty box, throw it out!

Wilson: What the hell happened in Baltimore?
House: Sorry, chief - I never kiss and tell.
Wilson: I think you just did.

Dr. Wilson: This isn't just going to go away.
House: No, but maybe you will.

Dr. Foreman: Hyper-vigilance, sudden irritability.
House: Symptomatic of...lunch with Cuddy?

House: I know you're in there. I can hear you caring.

House: (to Foreman) Your four weeks just expired. Your reign of terror is over – mine has just begun. Now go stick a needle up her hoo-hoo and find that cancer.
Dr. Chase: "Hoo-hoo"?
Dr. Foreman: He went to Hopkins.

Stella: What's wrong with your foot?
House: War wound.
Stella: Does it hurt?
House: Every day.
Stella: Is that why you're so sad?
House: Oh aren't you adorable. I'm not sad, I'm complicated - chicks dig that. One day you'll understand.

Stacy: What was Greg like after I left?
Dr. Cuddy: Uhh, an egomaniacal narcissistic pain in the ass. Same as before you left.
Dr. Cameron: You won't read your mail, but you'll open mine.
House: It was confidential. I wanted to know.
Dr. Cameron: The most important letter of my life, and you're still an ass.
House: Comforting, isn't it?

Dr. Foreman: It's the perfect marriage – there's nothing to fight about if you never talk about anything.

Dr. Wilson: Being miserable doesn't make you better than anyone else, House. It just makes you miserable.

House: You're gonna want to paralyze her. Run tests on a flailer and somebody's gonna lose an eye.

Dr. Wilson: Great, breaking up a marriage - fertile ground for high comedy.

# Distractions

This is the twelfth episode of the second season of House MD

## Synopsis

A father and son are tandem dirt-bike racing with the father driving. They pull to a stop and the son convinces him to switch places, but it ends up in disaster as the boy clasps the throttle and the bike goes out of control. The father is thrown clear from the vehicle and Adam crashes into some pipes, causing the bike bursts into flames.

Suffering burns on 40% of his body, the boy is rushed to the hospital. Low potassium levels, in combination with the severe burns, mean that Adam's prognosis is not terribly good. Meanwhile, Nurse Brenda approaches Dr. Cuddy and needs equipment for a lecture that a Dr. Weber is giving. Since Dr. Cuddy is not aware of any lecture, she concludes that House invited him. She confronts House, and is angered further when she learns that he gave a patient a migraine to test some new medication.

There is not enough skin left on top of Adam's chest to do an EKG and the staff does what it can to monitor him. The parents report he has smoked pot but isn't on any other drugs that they know of, and the father believes Adam crashed the bike due to some kind of muscle spasm. Adam goes into convulsions – House suspects MS so they test using a Doppler sound device.

Cuddy introduces her surprise guest Dr. Philip Weber, who specializes in headaches. House is lurking in the audience and Wilson recognizes him: he and House went to Hopkins, and House lost his chance to get an internship when Weber accused him of cheating. Now House is exacting revenge many years later, he's out to prove that Weber's a bad scientist.

Meanwhile, the staff uses images to check Adam's eye-response patterns, which reveals some indicators of internal bleeding, and Foreman enters the lecture to consult with House. Foreman and Chase try to locate the bleed while House needles Weber on his stated breakthrough, disputing Weber's study. Weber counters that the only way to disprove his study would be to use a live, conscious person. House induces a migraine on himself to test Weber's medicine. Weber's medicine doesn't work.

Adam, meanwhile seems to have an orgasm though he is unconscious, and they conclude that Adam's pain and pleasure receptors have been crossed. This is fortunate in terms of the fact that it may help with the burn pain but unfortunate in that it may be a sign of infection. House proposes they use maggots to eat the dead flesh from the burns, and Wilson plays armchair psychologist, accusing House of inducing a migraine to punish himself for letting Stacy go.

During this heated accusation, the maggots are gnawing away on the dead flesh of the burns but the brain irregularities are still present. House orders a risky lumbar puncture and Foreman reluctantly advises the parents to approve the test, causing marital strife when Adam's mother blames his father.

The spinal tap yields no useful information. They have no other way to test for the telltale lesions so House has the anesthesiologist wake him up. Adam is incredible pain and doesn't have the answers to any of the questions House asks, so the anesthesiologist knocks him back out. After taking a shower, House begins to hallucinate.

House meets with the staff and concludes that Adam was taking anti-depressants, which accounts for the seizure and excess seratonin. The extra seratonin is potentially lethal, but treatable. House wants to speak to Adam again but the parents have forbidden it lest he suffer. So House confronts the parents to determine if Adam was suffering from depression. The parents are sure he's told them everything, and since House still can't explain the orgasm, he goes into Adam's chamber over the parent's wishes.

Foreman intervenes but not before House notices a cigarette burn on Adam's arm. House opines that Adam was trying to quit smoking and using anti-smoking meds with anti-depressants in them, such as wellbutrin.

Later Cuddy confronts House and wants to know if he took LSD to cure his migraine. House admits he did and then took anti-depressants to short-circuit the hallucinations. Weber barges in and angrily accuses House of reporting to his corporate sponsors that his drug doesn't work and House acknowledges that he has, and now they are even.

He then goes home and enjoys a hired companion for the evening.

## Words of the day

Seratonin: This is neurotransmitter synthesized in the central nervous system of humans and animals. Serotonin is also found in many mushrooms and plants, including fruits and vegetables. It is believed to play an important role in the regulation of anger, aggression, mood, sleep, sexuality, and appetite. Low levels of serotonin have been associated with an increase in aggressive and angry behaviors, as well as other symptoms

## Memorable Quotes

Dr. Cuddy: (walking into House's office) Hey! Did you drop acid?
House: Why would I do that?
Dr. Cuddy: To annoy me. Or maybe because you're miserable, or because you want to self-destruct. Pick one.

House: Why is it so dark in here? It's a beautiful day outside. Open the shades, let the sun shine in.
Dr. Cameron: It's nighttime.
House: It's still Tuesday, right?

House: (to the parents) He has a cigarette burn on his wrist. Also a fading nicotine stain between two fingers. Bad news, your son has a filthy, unhealthy habit. Good news, he's trying to quit. Bad news, quitting is killing him. Good news, I can cure him. Bad news... no, that's the end of it.

House: I didn't know people actually read emails--the delete button is so conveniently located.

Dr. Wilson: (talking to House) Foolproof plan, by the way. Either his meds would work and you'd be in psychic pain because von Evil is going to be rich; or they wouldn't, and you got to be in agony all day. Perfect lose-lose situation. Very you.

Dr. Foreman: Hey, if you feel chest pain, you need to let me know. Verapamil can cause congestive heart failure.
House: Nothing can hurt my heart.

Dr. Foreman: Why didn't you take the patient to radiology, get an MRA?
House: Obviously I was doing something illegal. Using nuclear imaging would have raised questions.

House: God you're good! You're putting me to sleep!
Dr. Cuddy: You induced a migraine headache in a coma patient?

House: Gave him a little headache, similar to the one you're giving me now.
Cuddy: Have you even read an ethical guideline?

Dr. Wilson: This guy's name is Weber, not von Lieberman.
House: I call Weber "von Lieberman." Way eviler.

Weber: You cannot test this on an abnormal brain.
House: That's so close-minded, He's not "abnormal", he's special.
Dr. Cuddy: Cameron is worried about you. I told her that LSD lasts up to twelve hours. If you were functional she must be wrong.
Dr. House Either that or I also took a whole bunch of anti-depressants, which short-circuited the LSD... I'm just saying that would also explain it.

Dr. Wilson: (to a disgruntled House) Doctor Jekyll I presume? They found a half-eaten sheep in the zoo, and the police want to ask you a few questions.

Dr. Cameron: (Adam's) brain is like a waiter that's got too many...
House: Hey, hey... I do the metaphors.

Dr. Foreman: Been looking for you.
House: Been avoiding you.

Dr. Cuddy: Did you sign this?
House: Uh... yeah. We can talk later about the appropriate discipline.

Dr. Cameron: What are you looking for?
House: Same as you – love, acceptance, solid return on investment.
Dr. Wilson: So what's the plan – you're going to wait until he bends over and make a fart sound?
House: I'm not here about the past – he's a bad scientist.
Dr. Wilson: Well, you cheated off him – how bad could he be?
House: He got the answer wrong.

Dr. Wilson: You have got to find less debilitating outlets than humiliating people. I hear bowling is more fun than stalking.
House: But I'm better at this.

Weber: (to House) Who are you?
Dr. Wilson: (sotto voce) Just a lunatic who needs a hobby.

Weber: Do I know you?
House: I know your math skills -- they blow.
Dr. Wilson: Touché.

Dr. Cameron: Could pain medicine cause an orgasm?

House: I wish.

Dr. Foreman: House! You can't do this!

House: Oh, if I had a nickel for every time I've heard that.

House: The universe always settles the score.

Dr. Cuddy: Does it?

House: No, but it should.

# Skin Deep

This is the thirteenth episode of the second season of House, MD

## Synopsis

A teenaged runway model named Alex complains of nausea in the middle of a fashion show. The director, Austin, dismisses it, and her father, Martin, gives her anti anxiety meds and sends her on stage. She swallows them and seems to feel better for a moment but when she goes on stage, she sways, grabs on to another model, and collapses.

House wakes up, his leg in more pain than usual. At the hospital, Wilson suggests that the leg might actually be healing, and House may want to go into rehab for his Vicodin addiction. House refuses but quickly takes on the case of the teenaged supermodel. House suspects that the model drank or took drugs, and her father admits to giving her valium. Tests confirm it, and also alert the team to the presence of opiates. A state of rapid detox is induced. She first appears to suffer from withdrawal, and then flat lines.

This scares her father and he tries to withdraw his consent for the hospital's treatment, wanting a slower detox, but House talks him out of it. . House then attends to a clinic patient who is suffering sympathetic labor pains as his wife gives birth. Alex wakes up from the coma. She utters the same things over and over, and appears to be suffering from short-term amnesia and some kind of brain damage. House points out that she didn't flatline long enough to have sustained any brain injury, and then goes so far as to suggest that she has post-traumatic syndrome because Martin is abusing her. An MRI shows her brain is normal, lending weight to House's diagnosis.

House's leg pain continues, making him sick, and Cuddy must deal with the man with the sympathetic labor pains, who refuses to talk to her. Finally he admits that he is embarrassed because he seems to be developing breasts, and Cuddy gives the patient House's pager number. Foreman questions House on whether his pain is affecting his judgment and House admits it may be. This possibility doesn't prevent him, however, from confronting Martin directly. During the MRI, Alex starts to convulse, and House continues to needle Martin, accusing him of promoting his daughter using sexually charged language. If Martin loves his daughter, he continues, he has to be honest so they can diagnosis any psychological problems. Martin admits he has abused her but says he only did so once. House tells the staff but the MRI shows elevated proteins in her CSF, which disproves all their theories.

Cameron is particularly enraged when House says that they can't report Martin's confession due to doctor-patient confidentiality. House orders a brain biopsy and Cameron asks Cuddy how to proceed with the sexual abuse issue. Wilson administers a MRI while Cuddy confronts House about covering up child abuse. She orders House to cooperate or she'll fire him.

Wilson concludes that the MRI shows no improvement and ever the armchair psychiatrist, suggests Stacy's absence is the cause of House's excruciating pain in his leg. The brain biopsy come back negative and House wonders if she has a tumor. House comes up with a new "test" – he pinches the tube to cut off the IV drip and cut off the convulsions. It works, which is the upside; the downside is that she has cancer.

House goes to Cuddy to ask for a favor – a shot of morphine to deal with the pain, and shows her that there is massive deterioration of the thigh muscle tissue.

Alex goes into the MRI under Wilson's care but his diagnosis differs from House's: he concludes there's no cancer.  Undeterred, House concludes that Alex is subconsciously displaying fake symptoms and they give her a new IV of saline only. A social worker is meeting with Alex. Both she and her father deny the accusations of abuse, and since there is no evidence, nothing can be done. Cameron presses Alex about it. She describes the encounter as her getting him drunk and seducing him. Then she convulses.

A new theory emerges: Alex is a hermaphrodite. Alex has cancer on the left testicle, which never dropped, and she's a male-psuedo hermaphrodite and immune to testosterone. Alex and her father have some problems with the news.

House gives Cuddy an update on the case and then asks for another morphine shot and Cuddy admits to giving him a placebo before. Later, while House plays the piano he considers his Vicodin and tries to discard it, but eventually gives in.

## Words of the Day

Hermaphrodite: An organism that possesses both male and female sex organs. Historically the term hermaphrodite has also been used to describe ambiguous genitalia in individuals of unisexual species, especially human beings.

The broader term intersex is often used and is preferred by many such individuals and medical professionals.

Addiction: Most can agree on the definition of an addict—someone who has a chronic or reoccurring use of substances or activities despite being aware of the negative effects. There is a substantial amount of disagreement, however, as to the cause. Popular theories put the cause in a variety of places: on the addict him/herself for making bad choices, on bad genes, on cultural predispositions, or on biochemical processes. Many clinicians also characterize addiction as a disease.

## Memorable Quotes

Martin: This is obviously a joke. This is impossible!
House: No, a joke would be me calling you a homo. See the difference?

House: (examining Alex's mammogram) I knew the twins were real. Chase owes me.

Dr. Wilson:: Brilliant idea sending Stacy away. It's really done wonders for you.
House: Listen, none of this has anything to do with Stacy.

Dr. Wilson: Right. Giant coincidence you've gone completely off the rails since she left. Inducing migraines, worsening leg pain.
House: Aw, you miss Stacy too?

Dr. Cameron: Since when do you voluntarily go see patients?
House: Have you seen her?
Dr. Cameron: She's fifteen!
House: Yeah, but there's something about her, something in her eyes, a kind of maturity...
Dr. Cameron: Yeah, yeah, she's an old soul - this is creepy, even for you.

House: Two clinic hours says that those love apples are handcrafted by God.
Dr. Foreman: I thought you didn't believe in God.
House: I do now.

Dr. Wilson: How'd you get here?
House: By osmosis.

Dr. Cuddy: Teenage supermodel. Presented with double vision, sudden aggressive behavior, cataplexy...
House: You had me at "teenage supermodel".

Alex: I was passed out, but I wasn't. I, I knew what was going on, but I couldn't move or talk...
House Yeah, sounds like a medical thing. It's called cataplexy. Catfight and cataplexy on the catwalk. Cool.

Dr. Foreman: There's no age limit on addiction.
House: (popping a Vicodin) He's right.

House: I take it you're married.
George: (gestures to his wedding ring) You must be psychic.
House: You must be witty.

Dr. Foreman: Why would your mind go to abuse so fast?
House: I had a funny uncle.
Dr. Foreman: You were abused?
House: What? No! Why'd your mind go to that so fast? I just had a funny uncle. Great stories, always filthy.

House: Fine, arrest him. Use Cuddy's handcuffs.

Dr. Wilson: Heard you killed your supermodel.
House: Only for a minute.
Dr. Wilson: Just for my own clarity, how many more patients do you have to kill before you admit this leg thing might be a problem?
House: Three.

Dr. Wilson: (over a microphone) House, this is God.

House: Look, I'm a little busy right now. Not supposed to talk during these things. Got time Thursday?

Dr. Wilson: Let me check. Oh, I got a plague! How about Friday?

House: You'll have to check with Cameron.

Dr. Wilson: Oh, damn it! She always wants to know why bad things happen. Like I'm gonna come up with a new answer this time.

Dr. Cuddy: House!

House: Quick, God! Smite the evil witch!

Dr. Chase: Why does she need more protection than some crack whore shivering in the clinic waiting room?

Dr. Foreman: I think you're just afraid to piss House off.

Dr. Chase: There's that too.

Dr. Wilson: If you think it will help, the drugs will help. Power of the mind.

House: You're right. The more I talk to you, the more the pain floods back.

House: Did you check the pancreas?

Dr. Wilson: Oh come on – you're just making up organs now, aren't you?

# Sex Kills

This is the fourtheenth episode of the second season of House.

## Synopsis

A family is playing cards when the daughter, Amy, says she has stomach pains. Her father Henry takes her aside then begins to have some kind of seizure, and when he snaps out of it, has no memory of it happening.

He goes to the clinic, and meets with Foreman. Henry says he's had no previous symptoms or seizures. Foreman opines that Henry may have testicular cancer, but House notes a possible abscess in his brain, or possibly a STD.

House meets with Wilson and, noticing he's buying a box of chocolates, tries to hassle Wilson into admitting he's having an affair, which he denies. Then House has to deal with a clinic patient, Tony, who has an odd fascination with cows and keeps asking for a prescription for a tranquilizer.

Meanwhile, in Henry's corner of the world, Foreman talks to Henry about the possibility of an STD and Henry says he hasn't slept with anyone since he got divorced. Foreman believes him but House doesn't. He hustles Amy out of the room to talk to Henry without his daughter present. When she's gone, Henry admits he did have sex during a cheese-tasting festival with his wife after she had several affairs.

House starts giving him STD treatments and both Henry and House lie to Amy so she won't know her father may have had gotten an STD from her mother after her mother slept with other people. But then Henry starts choking and coughing up blood, and must be intubated.

The new symptoms conflict with both Foreman's and House's initial diagnoses-- lymphoma or STDs. House notices Henry's had acid reflux then theorizes Henry may have eaten unpasteurized goat cheese with bacteria, which multiplied in his stomach. House proceeds as if this were the final diagnosis, treating him for the bacteria, while still harassing Henry about his sex life. Henry goes into cardiac arrest and tests confirm he needs a heart transplant.

House goes to the transplant board but Henry is 65 so they do not approve. House, though admitting the board has a point, still signs Cameron's letter of appeal. Then he meets with Tony again, who claims that his cow kicked him in the ankle. Cameron and House work to find a possible heart donor and find the vegetative body of a 40-year-old woman who died in a car accident. Her heart is bad but better than nothing.

House meets with the woman's husband, and asks medical questions about her background before asking for his wife's heart. The donor committee declares her heart non-viable but Foreman notices the medical report says she has Hepatitis-C. House disputes the diagnosis based on the fact that her husband said she suffered from fever and stomach pains.

Ronald orders the ventilator to be shut down but House keeps it going, hoping to salvage her heart, and appeals to Cuddy. Amy seeks out Ronald and asks him for his donation. Ronald punches House in the gut...then agrees to let Henry have the heart.

Now House and his staff have to diagnose the vegetative woman's illness and run her through a MRI as Ronald observes. They find a cyst but it's not a gall bladder infection – House suspects a liver infection and orders a staggering amount of antibiotics, liberal with medication since patient viability is not an issue.

House returns to his patient with the bovine fixation, and Tony reveals that he needed the tranquilizers to deal with sexual arousal caused by his mother. So House gives him the medication without mandating he see a psychiatrist. Then he talks to Wilson who hypothetically agrees he might be having an affair and wants House's advice but House doesn't seem interested in providing a shoulder to cry on.

Laura—the car crash victim—has a heartbeat that is irregular and House orders them to stop the medication rather then render the heart unfit for use for Henry. Cameron suspects a toxin that targeted the liver and House goes to her house with Ronald. They finds hair dye, sleeping pills, and diet pills, all suggesting she lied to Ronald about something, but none of which explain her fever. They keep searching until Cameron finds photos of naked teenage boys in her desk. House figures she may have had gonorrhea which caused scarring of the liver. The tests confirm their diagnosis but it's possible that they won't be able to fix her in time to save Henry.

House goes ahead with the transplant anyway, hoping to treat Henry for gonorrhea once they've got him away from deaths' door, lying to Ronald to finagle the heart out of him. Cameron prepares to give Ronald the news that his wife was cheating on him, had a thing for teenage boys, and contracted gonorrhea, but he reveals that Laura was distant and he had a one-night stand where he got gonorrhea, which he thinks he gave to her.

The heart is still viable and Henry revives.

At home, House is making supper when Wilson arrives uninvited and unannounced. he's been kicked out by his wife—it turns out she was the one who was having the affair because he wasn't spending enough time with her.

## Words of the Day

Gonorrhea This is among the most common STDs in the world. Early symptoms include a pus or discharge from the genitals, and may advance to include fever and nausea. Some people, however, may not show any symptoms at all.

## Memorable Quotes

Dr. Wilson: Some people bottle up their feelings, have them come out as physical pain. Healthy human beings express feelings such as affection by giving gifts.
House: Gifts express guilt. The more expensive the expression, the deeper the guilt. That's a $12 box so that means you haven't slept with her yet, or she wasn't that good.

House: A disease that attacks his brain, heart, and testicles. I think Byron wrote about that.

House: (about a comatose woman) She's a fridge with a power out. You start poking around inside, the vegetable goes bad. No offense.

Dr. Cuddy: He's 66 years old.
House: He told me he was 65. Liar. I'm outta here.

Dr. Foreman: His right testicle is almost twice as big as his left.
House: Cool!

House: When guys have brain/crotch problems, it's usually the result of using one too much and the other too little.

Dr. Cameron: I thought we were wearing the wrong shoes for cancer.
House: We're wearing the wrong shoes for testicular cancer. They're perfect for lymphoma. Except Chase's – they're just goofy.

House: Norwegian chocolate. Frankly, you buy that stuff the terrorists win.

Dr. Wilson: It's not all about sex, House.

House: Really? When did that change?

House: Wilson! How long can you go without sex?
Dr. Wilson: How long can you go without annoying people?

Henry: I assume you've been in love?
House: Is that the one that makes your pants feel funny?

House: Cheese is the devil's plaything.

House: Key to a long life – exotic women, boring cheese.

House: If you really cared about me you'd find me a better corpse.
Dr. Cuddy: Don't you think that's a little manipulative?
House: No, it's hugely manipulative.

Dr. Cameron: We're going to cure death?
House: (laughs maniacally) I doubt it.

Ronald: I assume House is a great doctor?
Dr. Chase: Why would you assume that?
Ronald: Because if you're that big a jerk you're either great or unemployed.

House: So I have to wonder what could be more humiliating then someone calling your girlfriend a cow and not being metaphorical?

Dr. Cameron: She's positive for gonorrhea.
House: I think that's the first time those words have been uttered in joy.

# Clueless

This is the fifteenth episode of the second season of House, MD.

## Synopsis

A woman and her husband are engaging in sexual role-play, pretending he is a rapist, when suddenly he has problems breathing and she calls an ambulance.

House, meanwhile, is having difficulties at home, having taken on Wilson as an uninvited roommate.

At the hospital, the role-play couple, Bob and Maria, are discussing his symptoms and are open about their unique relationship. Their "open" marriage causes a buzz in the staff as they all pass judgment on it. Cameron is supportive and feels they are probably happily married, but House, of course, bets against her. This fascinating topic does not distract them from remembering that Bob is there not to discuss his sex life but to have his swollen throat diagnosed, and they theorize about the possible cause.

Later House is meeting with a patient, Vincent, who has herpes, and strenuously denies having sex with anyone but his wife. House then prescribes not only for Vincent, but also for his wife and her karate teacher. Cameron, still curious about Bob and Maria, asks Maria about their sexual role-playing and Maria says there's only so long a married couple can keep things interesting without it.

Bob's tests show lung scarring and reduced capacity but the cause is still unknown. Soon additional symptoms appear, and Bob finds himself furiously scratching at a rash that appears out of nowhere on his chest.

House and the staff are discussing Bob's symptoms in the men's room, for whatever reason . House orders a test to determine if he has been exposed to high amounts of certain kinds of metals, and a search of their house. While House spars with Wilson over their new life as roommates, Foreman finds plenty of ants at the house, but no metals. House orders treatment for lead poisoning nonetheless, and also tests for food allergies. Bob continues to get worse, complaining of extreme foot pain, and as if they didn't have enough to deal with, Vincent's wife wants to file a complaint.

Bob goes into breathing arrest again and vomits, necessitating that they trache him. Foreman strongly asserts that Bob has lupus but House still believes it's heavy metal poisoning. House continues to take advantage of Wilson's cooking skills at home, complaining all the while. House wonders if Maria is trying to kill Bob, ordering a search of their property without Maria's knowledge. House then asks probing questions, insinuating that Maria was trying to harm Bob. She agrees to let him search her purse and he finds nothing. Cameron vouches for her, believing she's innocent and Cuddy refuses House's ridiculous request to give her a highly illegal cavity search.

Undeterred, House watches Maria while Wilson babbles on and on about his ongoing divorce. As they discuss their personal lives, Bob has another respiratory arrest but then revives. House suspects the lupus treatment suppressed his bone marrow and left him unprotected against a viral infection. House orders interferon treatment against the viral infection, even though there may be potentially unpleasant side effects.

Then House meets with Vincent and his wife and informs her that despite the fact that she doesn't, at present, have any sores, she indeed has herpes and could spread the infection. When they fight, House says that it is possible to get it from a public toilet. Vincent accepts it first, so House concludes he had the affair. House sees their wedding ring and gets another idea. He orders a test for gold poisoning and orders Cameron to keep Maria out of the bathrooms.

House goes to his house to get something and sees that Wilson hired his old maid after his wife fired her. He notices with displeasure and then quickly retrieves his old wedding band. Maria insists on going to the bathroom over Cameron's objections just as House arrives. When she washes her hands, a reaction occurs. They all discover that there is a toxin on them that reacts to House's gold ring. It turns out that she had been using an uncommon arthritis medicine that has gold on it, and she sprinkled it on her husband's cereal.

Maria is arrested and Bob starts to respond to the treatment. House goes home. On the answering machine, there is a message from a landlord who is offering Wilson an apartment, which House erases.

## Words of the Day

Gold Poisoning: Exposure to gold in small amounts is harmless, however, ingesting more than a certain threshold can cause symptoms much like those caused by heavy metal poisoning.

# Memorable Quotes

Dr. Cameron: He’s gonna need a lung transplant.
House: He’s becoming more attractive by the minute, isn’t he?
Dr. Cameron: You’re pleased. You think you’ve proved every marriage is a mistake
House: Do I look pleased?

House: He's choking on his tongue, not his feet.

Dr. Chase: (about the couple's threesome) Another guy, or girl?
Dr. Cameron: Girl. His wife's college roommate.
Dr. Chase: If he's not happily married, I don't know who could be.

Dr. Wilson: You're kicking me out? After one night?
House: Why, you think we should try counseling first?

House: Is the ant big and red or small and black?
Dr. Foreman: Medium and brown
House: Halle Berry brown or Beyonce brown?
Dr. Cameron: Is there a difference?

Dr. Wilson: I was watching something.

House: No, you were about to watch something. I'm watching something. See the difference?

Dr. Wilson: Now why do you have a season pass to the New Yankee Workshop?
House: It's a complete moron working with power tools. How much more suspenseful can you get?

House: Chase, find out what the resort cooks with, if they repainted recently, or did any plumbing repairs.
Dr. Chase: I don't speak Spanish.
House: Then it'll be challenging.

Dr. Cameron: If you ask me, if two people really trust each other, a threesome once every seven years might actually help a marriage.
House: Okay, I say we stop the DDX and discuss that comment.

Dr. Cameron: What was I supposed to do, tie her up?
House: Why not – she likes that.

Charlotte: I am not having an affair with my daughter's karate instructor, and I did not give my husband herpes.
Dr. Cuddy: Find out where House is...

House: A sex fiend with a swollen tongue. Just think of all the places I can make Foreman search.

House: Good Lord, what is that smell?
Dr. Wilson: Stuffed pepper.
House: Stuffed with what? Vomit?

Dr. Wilson: (to House) I'll be out of your hair tomorrow...what's left of it.

Vincent: The only person I've had sex with is my wife.
House: Bummer.

Dr. Cuddy: (about House) He'd give his own mother herpes if it got him out of clinic duty.

Dr. Wilson: Don't you ever eat anything besides canned soup and peanut butter?
House: Don't you ever eat anything that doesn't look like it's been rolled onto your plate by a dung beetle?

House: You blow-dry your hair?
Dr. Wilson: Oh, sorry, did I wake you up?
House: (louder) You blow-dry your hair?!?
Wilson: Oh, sorry for caring how I look like.
House: I think the word you're looking for is "obsessing."

# Safe

This is the sixteenth episode of the second season of House MD.

## Synopsis

Dan comes over to a girl's house to visit. Before he sees her, however, he has to make sure he has been thoroughly sanitized, and wear a mask. When he finally sees Melinda, she insists Dan remove her mask and he reluctantly agrees, and kisses her. About two minutes later, her skin blisters and she goes into respiratory distress until her mother rushes in and gives her an injection.

House is called to deal with the patient, and he and his staff determine Melinda had a heart transplant and has been in a sterile environment for six months. House, as usual, is skeptical when he hears that Melinda's reaction occurred when she was in a sterile environment. Cameron and Chase go over the house to verify that it is sterile, and surmise that Dan may have snuck in a window and had sex with Miranda at some point. A sperm sample from Dan, however, determines that his semen is not responsible for her reaction. Ever skeptical, House confronts Dan until he gets him to admit that he took penicillin for a week, and House points out she was allergic to it. By the time they tested his semen, the penicillin had been out of his system.

After House decides not to tell the parents, Melinda goes into a seizure and the team tests for congestive heart failure but the tests prove clean. Melinda gets increasingly stressed about the possibility of losing her transplanted heart.

Wilson arrives home to find that House has left a stethoscope on the door, indicating he's "not to be disturbed." House finally lets him in hours later. They discuss the case but Wilson ends up getting distracted due to his frustration at his home life.

At the hospital, Foreman and the parents discover that Miranda is not in the hospital bed. They conclude she's gone outside and Foreman heads for the roof and finds her halfway up the stairs. He listens to her tearful diatribe about her over protective mother, and her fears of losing her transplanted heart, and finally she agrees to go downstairs but Foreman notices her left foot is dragging. He then notices a muscle twitch and fears that it is an early indicator of paralysis.

House returns home where Wilson confronts him about the missing voice mails and House admits he erased the messages to keep Wilson there, and tells him he should stay until the divorce is final.

Melinda is getting progressively worse and refuses to see Dan. She is intubated when the paralysis reaches her lungs, and House concludes she has botulism. Melinda's parents, upset at their daughter's worsening condition, take the staff off the case and put Cuddy in charge. Undeterred, House questions Melinda further. The information she gives him leads him to believe that Dan may have picked up a tick from the tall grasses he routinely walks through, and passed it to her. . House searches for ticks while Melinda has another attack and Cuddy transfers Melinda to the ICU.

En route to the ICU, Foreman takes Melinda into the elevator where House is waiting. House shuts down the elevator and starts looking for the ticks again, fighting off Foreman's protests and physical restraints, all the while insisting that they need to treat the cause, not the symptoms. Working together, they revive her then look for the ticks. They find nothing. House realizes where the tick could be – in her vagina. With it located, she is finally able to be treated.

Melinda is ready to be discharged and Barbara manages to be less protective, telling her she will now be able to go to school. House arrives home and he and Wilson share the couch. Wilson admits he's finally called a divorce lawyer.

## Words of the Day

Tick: Tick is the common name for the members of the arachnid family. Ticks are external parasites, sucking the blood of mammals, birds, and occasionally reptiles and amphibians. Ticks are also vectors of a number of diseases.

## Memorable Quotes

Dan: What, do you think there was still some on my lips? I brushed my teeth.
House: Think lower and more fun.

Dan: Do you have to tell her (her seizure) was my fault?
House: No. Great part of being a grownup, you never have to do anything.
House: Lying to your parents is usually the right thing to do, but there is the impending death exception.

House: You wake up in the morning, your paint's peeling, your curtains are gone, and the water's boiling. Which problem do you deal with first?
Dr. Foreman: House...
House: None of them, the building's on fire!

Dr. Chase: We're going to need a semen sample. You can use the bathroom over there.
Dan: Right...uh...how do I...
Dr. Cameron: Aim and shoot.
Dr. Chase: No thinking about Dr Cameron--we'll know.

Dr. Chase: Melinda's dying.
House: We're all dying. How fast?

House: Get an L.P. And do PCRs for the viruses. And get an E.M.G. to check for Guillain-Barré. If Foreman's right we gotta find out why she's paralyzed. (team stare at House) But not before staring at me dumbly for a few seconds...

(House stops Foreman from writing on the whiteboard)
House: Sorry, there's a reason they call it the whiteboard. It's not my rule.
Dr. Foreman: We explained the anaphylaxis...
House: What do you mean we? I did!
At least I thought I did. Maybe I didn't. Still it was all me!

Dr. Foreman: I say we assume House was right about the anaphylaxis...
House: It is tempting.

Dan: But, you know, they've tested Melinda, they said she wasn't allergic to my stuff.
House: Yeah, four days later. By that time the penicillin was crusting up a sock in the bottom of your hamper.

Dr. Cameron: (to Chase) Too bad it's not you giving the (sperm) sample. We'd be done by now.

Dan: Is he Okay?
House: He's just tired from being in a coma so long.

House: What did he do to protect her? Brillo Pad his privates?
Cameron: I assume he washed, and he...
House: Oh, good work! Assumptions are so much faster than actual questions!

House: Everything sucks. Might as well find something to smile about.

Dr. Wilson: You erased my messages?
House: Yep. Decided I wanted you to stay. Told you that, didn't I?

Dr. Wilson: You're miserable and you're lonely and you're gonna trap me here to keep me every bit as miserable and lonely too.
House: Yeah. You're happy, happy, happy.

Dr. Wilson: You said you'd hang the stethoscope if you were having sex.
House: I didn't say it had to be with another person.

Dr. Foreman: (to Cameron) So I hear you don't want teenagers having sex. Teen suicide isn't high enough for you?

Dr. Wilson: Oh, no wonder you were in the mood - this month's New Jersey Journal of Cardiology.
House: Have you seen the centerfold? There's no way those valves are real!

House: What are you doing?!
Dr. Wilson: What? You asked me...
House: You knew that I was interested - that gives you a valuable bargaining chip. You'd have me doing dishes for a week!

House: Only way to confirm this, inject the rat with her blood and wait for it to get all botulistic on your ass. In the meantime, I'm going downstairs to browbeat a scared, dying teenage girl until she breaks down like...a scared, dying teenage girl.

Dr. Wilson: Cuddy called.
House: I know. I saw the caller ID.
Dr. Wilson: Young girl, anaphylactic shock.
House: You answered?
Dr. Wilson: Turns out, that's what stops the ringing.

House: Six months without putting out – Dr. Cuddy doesn't need to wear thong panties. It's not our call.
Dr. Cuddy: I was wondering when you'd get around to my panties.

Dr. Cuddy: These are your big ideas – somebody's lying?
House: Hasn't let me down yet.

Dr. Cameron: You had unsafe sex? The whole "unsafe" thing didn't tell you something?

Dr. Cameron: Love is an emotion certain people experience. Similar to happiness. You know, maybe I should give a more relatable example.
House: Ohhh...snap!

Dan: I mean, it can go through your stuff?

House: Totally, dude. There's this administrator here, whenever she gets sick she just gives me the prescription.

House: What's the good news, what's the bad news?

Dr. Chase: Congestive heart failure.

House: Is which?

Dr. Chase: Good news.

House: Why?

Dr. Chase: I don't know. Just... sounded like you.

# All In

This is the seventeenth episode of the second season of House, MD

## Synopsis

At a giant heart exhibit at a children's museum, a young boy named Ian asks to go to the restroom. It turns out, he is actually bleeding out of his anus. Just as the teacher notices, she starts experiencing contractions.

The clinic's charity poker tourney is interrupted as Ian is brought in and is initially assigned to Cuddy. Cuddy, however, has a good hand and House doesn't, so he goes to see Ian. His first instinct is to conclude that his brain is losing connection to his body. He says the case is somewhat like the case of a 73-year old woman from 12 years ago, and predicts Ian will have kidney failure, and then die.

Chase disagrees. He reminds House of the time he checked out a patient with similar symptoms but it turned out he didn't have the same illness. He goes on to assert that

House is obsessed with the case and sees the symptoms everywhere as a result of this obsession.

While examining the boy, Foreman finds nothing that would explain the bleeding. House orders a kidney biopsy, and determines that his kidneys are shutting down as predicted.

Foreman wants to call in Cuddy as Ian is her patient, but House hangs on to the case. As the tests continue, Foreman and Cameron report they found a small mass on the pituitary gland. This usually would indicate lymphoma but the tests for lymphoma show negative. House then breaks into the cafeteria to steal coffee while blithely predicting the next symptom, liver failure, will commence in about an hour and a half. House orders any and all possible treatments then calls Wilson so he can help him win, and Cuddy will want to stay at the table and gamble.

At first, the liver continues to function but Ian's platelet count drops. This is regarded as a good sign since it was unexpected and perhaps represents another ailment that won't kill the boy. Ian goes into respiratory distress and House calls Wilson. He finally comes up when House tells him what's going on, and that an oncology expert is called for, and tries to determine why their interferon treatment caused the respiratory distress. Wilson determines that Ian might have Kawasaki's, at first, but tests for this disease turns up negative. They do, however, see a small mass in his heart, and as House probes the heart, Ian goes into coronary failure. They manage to revive him after eight minutes. House continues the probe.

Cuddy soon gets bored of the game and leaves to go take her patient away from House. House, nonetheless, orders a test for Erdheim-Chester, which they've already tested for and proved negative.

House stubbornly insists on the test anyway, betting that it hadn't shown up because at the time, it hadn't reached Ian's gastro-intestinal tract yet but now it's active. It turns out positive. They give Ian the proper treatment and he revives.

## Word of the Day

Erdheim-Chester This is a very rare disease that usually manifests itself in middle age. Diagnosis can be challenging because the symptoms are so diverse, but usually include bone pain and wasting.

## Memorable Quotes

House: The parents are mad because their kid is dying, it's understandable, but if he doesn't die they won't be mad anymore.
Dr. Cuddy: But if he's brain damaged they might still be a little ticked.

House: Can anyone think of a reason why Kawasaki's can't affect the elderly, other than it doesn't?

Dr. Chase: Meds seem to be working, liver's holding it's own.
House: Good.
Dr. Chase: But the platelets are dropping.
House: Even better.
Dr. Chase: Why? It means he's getting sicker.
House: New is good... because the old ended in death.

Dr. Wilson: Obsession is dangerous.
House: Only if you're on a wooden ship and your obsession is a whale. I think I'm in the clear.

Dr Wilson: You can't use another patient's lab to diagnose Kawasaki disease!
House: Is that like a dare or something?

Dr. Chase: I'm going to do a biopsy.
House: Forget it! That battle is over. His raising creatine is his kidneys' way of saying "go on without me."

Dr. Chase: What are you doing?
House: What we came here to do
Dr. Chase: But he almost died
House: I know, I was here.

Dr. Chase: I vote for neurofibromitosis.
House: Why?
Dr. Chase: Because the other choices suck worse.

Dr. Cuddy: Call.
House: You'll call anything.
Dr. Cuddy: My stack's bigger than your stack. You in or out?
House: Relative to their size, gorillas have smaller testicles than humans.
Dr. Cuddy: Well, then you'd probably have an edge over a gorilla. But not over me.
House: Reason is, primate testes size inversely corresponds to the fidelity of our females
Dr. Wilson: You think there might be a better time to annoy me about my wife?
House: I'm talking about poker.
Dr. Wilson: Right.

Dr. Cuddy: Women are evil, you're right to drive them away. Call, fold, or raise!

House: Hey, how's that anal fissure? Did it heal yet, or is it still draining? Oh, I'm sorry, I didn't realize he came back for seconds. I figured that after that girl in the stairwell you'd be done for the night.
Dr. Chase: He's joking.
House: No Adam's apple, small hands. No surprises this time.
Michelle: I'll...see you later. (leaves)
House: I've got a case.
Dr. Chase: Well, you could have just said that. You didn't need to screw with me.
House: Yeah, if I didn't screw with you , you'd spend the whole night thinking you might get laid, which means you'd be useless. Better to extinguish all hope.

Dr. Wilson: If you're going to mess with me, wouldn't it be more fun to do it in person.
House: (on the cell phone) Yes, it would.

House: When you were wearing your "Frankie says relax" t-shirts, I was treating a 73 year old woman who went through this progression of symptoms. The last of which was death. And in case any of you missed that class in med school, that one's untreatable.

Ian: I have a question, and I need to go to the bathroom.

Teacher: What would you like to do first.

Ian: Question.

Teacher: Okay.

Ian: Where's the bathroom?

Dr. Wilson: Are you going to call?

House: You know, relative to its size, the barnacle has the largest penis of any animal.

House: These procedures would be so much easier if you could do them on healthy people.

House: I raise.

Dr. Wilson: So are you going to tell me an annoying story every time I raise?

House: God, that would be annoying.

## Sleeping Dogs Lie

This is the seventeenth episode of the second season of House, MD

## Synopsis

A woman named Hannah is trying to go to sleep with no luck, and pours herself a glass of wine. In the morning, her roommate finds that she has overdosed on sleeping pills, and takes her to the clinic.

When she arrives, House learns that she hasn't slept in 10 days, even though she took sleeping pills. Cameron is busy complaining about the fact that Foreman wrote about one of her cases, potentially plagiarizing her work, when House interrupts to suggest an optical disease that is disrupting signals to Hannah's brain.

Cameron tests her optic nerve and Hannah dozes off for 10 seconds in the middle of the test, but when she snaps out of it, she doesn't remember nodding off. House wants to stress her brain by keeping her in an uninterrupted state of wakefulness, and the staff takes shifts to make sure she doesn't sleep. Then she starts bleeding rectally and they have to give her a colonostomy—a painful procedure--without giving her a sedative. In the middle of the test she gets a nosebleed.

The test of the nasal blood gives no new or useful information, and Cameron and Foreman argue over what's wrong with her. House notices that the patient was exposed to poison ivy at about the same time she stopped sleeping, and orders a treatment for Wegener's.

He then goes to visit a patient at the clinic named Mrs. Ling, who wants birth control pills for her PMS. House concludes she has a cold and the daughter Anne, who speaks English, is the one trying to get the pills.

When Hannah goes into rapid eye movement but is completely oblivious to it, House figures the treatment for her poison ivy suppressed her allergy to the dog her friend gave her a month ago.

Under pressure, Hannah complains that she is tired of Max, the friend that gave her the dog, and is secretly planning to break up with her. As she continues talking she mentions that she has back pain and Cameron discovers evidence of internal bleeding. Foreman announces that the tests show her liver has shut down, and unless she gets a transplant, Hannah only has six hours left. Even if she does get the liver, they still won't know what's wrong with her and will have to run more tests. Max volunteers her liver as soon as she hears the news.

Now that they have 36 extra hours, and House overrides Cameron's concerns about the ethical dilemma—Max doesn't know that her partner is planning on breaking up with her, and if she did, might change her mind and choose not to donate. House goes to Cuddy to get permission for the transplant. Cuddy does what she can to convince Max of the risks but she's willing to go through it to save her partner.

Meanwhile, Cameron puts pressure on Hannah to tell Max. Wilson opines on the situation wherein Cameron has accused Foreman of stealing her article, taking the middle road and admitting that Foreman probably should have checked with Cameron first. House dismisses Wilson's concerns while Cameron gets Hannah and Max alone. House, concerned that Cameron might let the cat out of the bag and warn Max about the impending breakup, interrupts them to sedate Hannah.

Despite a few complications during the course of the surgery, Max recovers and Hannah tests negative for cancer. To figure out what the problem is, they have to turn off the immuno-suppressant drugs to get a clear reading on what her problem might be.

At the clinic, Mrs. Ling and Anne are back. In Mandarin, House tells the mom that the daughter is taking birth control pills.

As for Hannah, she has nodes under her arm that indicate she got what is colloquially known as the Black Plague from fleas on dog she was given. They order treatment while Cameron finds out that Max knew about Hannah leaving her all the time, and figures donating the liver might get her to stay.

Cameron approaches Foreman and suggests they both apologize, but Foreman points out they're not really friends, merely colleagues, and he doesn't have anything to apologize for.

## Words of the Day

The Black Plague: This disease, practically unheard of now in the modern-day industrialized world, wiped out large portions of Europe's population in the 1300s, and recurred throughout the Dark Ages.

## Memorable Quotes

House: I need a little help.
Dr. Cuddy: Inexplicable rash on a patient's scrotum you need me to look at?

Dr. Cameron: You have to sedate a patient to do a colonoscopy.
House: Why? Because of all the pain?

House: So he sleeps, but she just can't stay asleep.
Dr. Foreman: You going somewhere with this?
House: You know what keeps me up at night...? Monsters in the closet.
Dr. Foreman: There's no monsters in the closet, we looked.
House: Certainly not showing up on the scanner.

Dr. Cuddy: She took the pills to sleep, not to kill herself.
House: Clever alibi.

Dr. Foreman: So the butt bleed's just a nose bleed.
Dr. Cameron: That much blood is not "just a" anything.
House: When two people fight this much, you know what it means.

Dr. Foreman: It's gotta be a massive sinus hemorrhage that was draining down her throat and out the back.
Dr. Cameron: The question isn't what, it's why.
House: Oh, get a room!

House: (to a Chinese girl translating for her mother) I'd say her problem is more likely a URI, than a PMS.
Anne: URI?
House: Upper Respiratory Infection, a cold.
Anne: I-I don't think so.
House: I also think she's got a problem with SAC.
Anne: SAC?
House: Thanks for playing. Stupid American Child. If you want the pill, all you have to do is to walk into any health clinic in Jersey, alone and ask for it.

Cuddy: Twenty-five-year-old female with sleep issues.
House: I'm guessing she's... what's the medical term? Upset. These 25-year-old females are usually completely rational. They're rocks. Really.

Dr. Cameron: Lovely. Revenge as motive for success.
Dr. Cuddy: Well, it doesn't have to be the motive. But it sure tastes good.

Dr. Cameron: If we want this to not get in the way of our friendship, I think we both have to apologize and put it behind us.
Dr. Foreman: I like you, really...we have a good time working together. But ten years from now, we're not gonna be hanging out, having dinners. Maybe we'll exchange Christmas cards, say "Hi," give a hug if we're at the same conference...we're not friends, we're colleagues...and I don't have anything to apologize for.

Dr. Cameron: We're withholding information relevant to her decision to risk her life! How is that not an ethical dilemma?
House: It's not medical information.
Dr. Cameron: Who cares?
House: The AMA.

Dr. Cuddy: (waking House up) You've seen one patient in the last two hours!
House: Complicated case. I'm a night owl, Wilson is an early bird: we're different species.
Dr. Cuddy: Move him into his own cage!
House: Who'd clean up the droppings from mine?

Dr. Cameron: If she talks, if she does the decent thing then you don't get to solve your puzzle, your game's over, and you lose.

House: Yeah. I want to save her. I'm morally bankrupt.

House: Given the choice of life versus death, those bad, bad people are going to choose life.

House: I'm saying 'I don't care what they do as long as my life isn't interrupted by pointless conversations like this one.'

House: It's only moral to save a person if they love you? That's kind of a selfish way at looking at life. I like Wilson's disease, I like cancer, I love mushrooms.

Dr. Cameron: (to House) Okay, well we can either base our diagnosis on your admittedly keen understanding of lesbian relationship or we could do a scratch test.

House: You, on the other hand, continue to be flabbergasted every time someone actually acts like a human being. Foreman did what he did because it worked out best that way for him. That's what everyone does.
Dr. Cameron: That is not the definition of being human. That's the definition of being an ass.

Dr. Cameron: Right, we're both victims. A simple heads up, that's all I needed. Maybe between your incredibly witty

remarks about anal sex and Cuddy's breasts you could've tipped me off.
House: Then I'd have Foreman pissed off... and as annoying as you can be, at least I know you're not gonna pop a cap in my ass. Witty, huh?

House: (to Chinese mother about Anne) Not the sharpest chopstick in the drawer, is she?

House: We can only hope Cameron learned something from this.
Dr. Wilson: Right. Because you're all about the teaching.
House: Our children...are the future.

Dr. Cameron: You're on his side?
Dr. Cuddy: Sides? This isn't dodgeball.

Dr. Cameron: You can't ask the person she's about to dump to donate half her liver!
House: It does seem tacky, doesn't it?

Dr. Cameron: Do you have any idea what it feels like to have a 6' hose shoved into your large intestine?
House: No. But I now have a much greater respect for whatever basketball player you dated in college.

Dr. Cameron: Depriving her of even the few minutes of sleep she does have, it's torture.
House: So is cutting people with knives, but you can totally get away with that if you have a doctor coat on.

House: If it has anything to do with who made the mistake, I don’t care. If it has to with me making a mistake, I really don't care.

(Cameron, Foreman, and Chase come in)
Dr. Cameron: We've got rectal bleeding.
House: What, all of you?

Hannah: I've got the plague?
House: Don't worry, it's treatable. Being a bitch, though...nothing we can do about that.

# House Versus God

This is the eighteenth episode of season two of House MD.

## Synopsis

A young faith healer, Boyd, makes a great show of channeling God so that a woman can walk. But as Boyd warns the congregation of fire and damnation, and tries to lead them down a path to the Almighty, he has a series of spasms and collapses to the ground.

Wilson attempts to collect some things from House's apartment, slightly miffed because House prefers that he not attend his weekly poker party. Meanwhile, Cameron and Foreman are testing Boyd as he claims to have the ability to converse directly with God, attempting to prove it by telling Cameron and Foreman that he knows about their ongoing spat. The tests show low sodium and diluted urine. House, an atheist, is unimpressed with Boyd's close friendship with our Lord and Savior. House orders preliminary treatment and goes to talk to Boyd. Boyd is chatty and clearheaded, and they speak briefly before House notices he's drinking water from a previously opened bottle.

Wilson, meanwhile, is tending to a cancer patient, Grace, who wants to go off of her pain medicine. House interrupts for a consult to basically confirm his own theory and rant about people's beliefs and perceptions of God. Boyd wakes up and starts meandering through the halls, singing hymns, pausing to take a sip from the drinking fountain. As Chase leads him back to his bed, Boyd sees Grace and lays his hands upon her.

House decides to give Boyd an MRI when Wilson interrupts his meeting to express his irritation with Boyd: Grace is now convinced she is healed and is in for a shocker and a downer when she inevitably discovers she is not. Later Boyd comes in to talk with House who scolds him for playing with people's emotions, and Boyd talks about what God has said to him about House. He concludes by informing House that God wants him to invite Wilson to his poker game.

Wilson, when confronted, insists to House that he did not tell Boyd about the poker game. The MRI shows evidence of tubular sclerosis and they prepare to operate – House believes the growth is responsible for Boyd's symptoms. Surgery is called for, but Boyd and his father, Walter, both flatly refuse the surgery. Displaying an uncanny ability for manipulation, Wilson almost convinces Boyd that if he's truly a saint then his humility would lead him to agree to the tests.

At his house that night, House is playing the piano when Wilson tells him the shocking news that Grace's tumor is smaller. House demands all of her records and orders her to be kept away from Boyd but she disregards her advice. House decides that the only way Boyd will agree to the surgery is if they somehow can prove to Boyd that Grace is not healed. The staff now tries to figure out why her tumor might have shrunk, and checks out her home.

In the midst of his search mission at Grace's, Chase is narrowly caught by her boyfriend. House, meanwhile, on a winning streak at the table, figures that Grace told Boyd about the poker game when she learned it from Wilson. She learned it from Wilson, House realizes, because he slept with her.

Boyd is preparing to check out with his father's permission while Wilson storms out after accusing House of hating religion. A charge that House agrees with until Wilson, in his typical armchair psychiatrist mode, opines that House hates religion because he has to be in control of everything all the time. They're interrupted because they are informed that Boyd is running a fever. House concludes the tubular sclerosis isn't responsible and it's time for a spinal tap to do further tests, but Boyd refuses again. . They appeal to Walter but he prefers to leave it in God's hands.

House then realized what happened. Boyd has a strain of the herpes virus that he gave to Grace, which attacked her tumor and caused it to go into temporary remission. House finally gets Walter to order Boyd to undress and they find that he does, indeed, have herpes and is in the midst of an outbreak.

Later Boyd meets with House and wishes him good luck with his life of certainty. Grace is still happy even though the cancer is coming back. And House and Wilson are getting along again.

## Words of the Day

Faith Healing: The use of spiritual means in treating disease, sometimes accompanied with the refusal of modern medical techniques. The term is sometimes used to describe those Christians who are under the impression that God heals people through the power of the Holy Spirit. In clinical trials, faith healing was shown to be absolutely ineffective.

## Memorable Quotes

Dr. Chase: You say "won the lottery," he says "miracle."
House: Yeah, the hand of God reached into this kid's pants, made him have sex, so he could scratch a rash, stick his fingers into some woman's face, and give her a few extra months. Come on, it's just another liar and manipulator.
Dr. Wilson: Well nobody's as perfect as you are.

Dr. Foreman: His fever is 103° and rising, if we don't do something real soon, he's going to be chatting with God face-to-face real soon.

Dr. Wilson: Did you remember my DVD player?
House: If you wanted it, you shouldn't have left it behind when you moved out.
Dr. Wilson: Oh! I get it, it's a drag watching porn on VHS.
House: I'll call you as soon as I'm done with it.

Dr. Foreman: So, you believe God might exist but you don't think about it? It's the most important issue ...
Dr. Cameron: I think penguins might as well speculate about nuclear physics. Why are we having this conversation?
Dr. Foreman: What? I'm curious.

Dr. Cameron: You cannot tell someone they're your colleague, and not a friend, and then casually chat about the afterlife.

House: Faith; that's another word for ignorance, isn't it? I've never understood how people can be so proud of believing in something with no proof at all, like that's an achievement.

House: I fear for the human race. A teenager claims to be the voice of God and people with advanced degrees are listening.

House: You know, I get it that people are just looking for a way to fill the holes; that they want the holes; they want to live in the holes; and they go nuts when someone else pours dirt in their holes. Climb out of your holes, people!

Dr. Chase: How long have you been healing people?
Boyd: You believe that's what I'm doing?
Dr. Chase: I'd like to.
Boyd: But you don't. Why do you always do things you don't want to do? It's okay; I don't expect a real answer.

House: Half the doctors who specialize in oncology turn into burnt-out cases but you... you eat neediness.
Dr. Wilson: Lucky for you.

House: (to Wilson) You're a functional vampire. Sure, you're heroic and useful to society but only because it feeds you. (

Boyd: God says you look for excuses to be alone.
House: See, that is exactly the kind of brilliance that sounds deep, but you could say it about any person who doesn't pine for the social approval of everyone he meets, which you were cleverly able to deduce about me by not being a moron. Next time tell God to be more specific.
Boyd: God wants you to invite Dr. Wilson to your poker game.

Boyd: Dad? You have to have faith in me...
Walter: I have faith in the Lord. You, I trust... as much as you can trust a teenage boy.

Dr. Wilson: And that's why religious belief annoys you. Because if the universe operates by abstract rules you can learn them, you can protect yourself. If a Supreme Being exists he can squash you any time he wants.
House: He knows where I am. (

(doing introductions)
House: Wilson! This is Dry Cleaner Guy. Tax Accountant. Guy from the bus stop. This is Wilson.

Dry Cleaner: How come he gets a name?
House: Seniority.

House: Don't talk to my patient.
Dr. Wilson: What are you talking about?
House: You get all huffy when my patient stumbles into yours in the hallway, but you've got no qualms about chatting my guy up.
Dr. Wilson: This is fun, it's like Password. Keep talking, I'll jump in when I get a clue what the hell you're talking about.

Dr. Wilson: House! Why the hell did you let an unstable patient wander the hallways?!?
House: His leash broke.

House: Isn't it interesting that religious behavior is so close to being crazy we can't tell it apart.

House: He is not a saint. He figures out what's going on in people's lives by watching, listening, deducing...
Dr. Wilson: And you're worried about trademark infringement?
House: Then he passes on advice from God so he can watch them jump. It's a power trip.
Dr. Wilson: Ah, and there the similarities end.

House: So, you're a faith healer? Or is that a pejorative? Do you prefer something like "divine health management"?

Dr. Chase: You're going to talk to a patient?
House: God talks to him. It'd be arrogant of me to assume I'm better than God.

House: God ever talk to you when you were in the seminary?
Dr. Chase: Ummm... no.
House: God's loss, our gain.

House: God talks to him!
Dr. Chase: It's not psychosis, he's just religious, the only medical issue that showed up on the blood work is low sodium.
House: No - you talk to God, you're religious. God talks to you - you're psychotic.

House: Got to go – building full of sick people. If I can hurry, maybe I can avoid them.

Boyd: The nurses talk about you a lot.
House: Ah, don't believe them – I keep a sock in my pants.

Dr. Wilson: Excuse me – I have a friend with...boundary issues. (

Dr. Wilson: Can this wait five minutes?
House: Is she dying?
Dr. Wilson: Yes...
House: Before the end of this consult?
Dr. Wilson: They could build monuments to your self-centeredness.

House: You would let this kid die just to get into a stupid poker game?
Dr. Wilson: You'd let him die to keep me out?

Dr. Chase: (to House) The honor of working for you is not worth a felony charge.

Dr. Wilson: House, you are...as God made you.

Dr. Foreman: God would probably want you to take the stick out of your butt and get over this.
Dr. Cameron: If there is some higher order running the universe, it's probably so different from anything our species can conceive there's no point in our even thinking about it. But I doubt He gives a damn about my butt.

# Euphoria Part One

This is the eighteenth episode of the second season of House MD.

## Synopsis

Two policemen pursue a suspect they refer to as Baby Shoes, and he hides in a trash can  at a dead end. One of the cops, Joe, is instructed to look in the trash can, but he laughs uncontrollably as he approaches the garbage can, even continuing to laugh as the criminal goes for his gun, shoots him, and runs. Joe, the happy cop, lies in a pool of his own blood and laughs.

As Foreman's father gives him an enthusiastic congrats on the article he stole from Cameron, House interrupts with the cop's case, reporting that in addition to the laughter, he has high CO levels. House orders him put into a hyperbaric chamber while Foreman checks out the cop's home. It is a complete mess. He takes samples of some of the disgusting, moldy items lying around the place, and stumbles upon a room with rows of potted marijuana plants.

House checks out the precinct and notices a cop coughing near an air conditioner. He returns and just as the group convenes with their various opinions, the cop's condition appears to improve. Just in cast, they conduct more tests and to their surprise, conclude that Joe has gone blind. They wonder if bullet fragments are responsible but can't do a MRI without making sure they have completely pulled out the bullets. They administer an angio. Meanwhile, Foreman's issues with the police become more and more apparent. Further complicating things, the bullet appears to be ferrous.

House decides to shoot a corpse to test how the MRI will affect it. As they check, Foreman seems to take the case less and less seriously. They run the MRI and the bullets are pulled out through the corpse's skull.

The MRI is now damaged from the bullet, and will be out of commission for two weeks, so they resort to ultrasound to look for clots. Joe starts bleeding from the eyes and Foreman starts to laugh hysterically. They conclude that somehow, the disease has been transmitted to Foreman, and quarantine him with Joe. House brings in a portable MRI to scan Foreman's head and starts taking blood tests from the staff. They find a lesion near the center of the brain that controls euphoria but have no idea what could have caused it. House also wonders why Cameron is so willing to forgive Foreman for stealing her article now that he's sick.

Chase takes samples from Foreman, who is insistent on being involved in forming a diagnosis in spite of the fact that he is sick and in a plastic tent. House wants to do a biopsy on Joe's brain but the previous treatment prevents them from doing so. House plans to do the biopsy on Foreman and he eventually capitulates, but only if he is also treated for the staph infection that he suspects he has. They insert an oyama reservoir to administer the anti-staff medicine and House decides to do his biopsy while he's in there.

The tests prove negative and House orders more tests but refuses to let anyone go to Joe's apartment for reasons that are unclear. Joe is starting to experience more and more pain and Foreman wonders why the biopsy is inconclusive. Foreman insists that Cameron or someone should go to the apartment. She refuses. He sticks her with a needle, exposing her. He tells her she has to either go to the apartment, or end up in quarantine along with him and Joe.

While House and Chase go over the tests and Joe is in increasing pain, Cameron breaks into the apartment wearing a hazmat suit. Foreman administers more morphine to Joe, putting him dangerously close to death, but it wears off in literally thirty seconds, and as Foreman looks on in horror, Joe screams in pain because the damage has spread to the pain center of the brain. They put Joe into a coma. House, realizing that Foreman hasn't asked where Cameron is, suspects that she went to the apartment.

House goes to Joe's apartment and confronts Cameron, telling her that the chance of infection from the needle is small. He takes the samples she's gathered and notes the three loaves of bread on the counter. It appears that he has been feeding the pigeons on his patio. Cameron finds the bucket where Joe has been collecting the pigeon poo to use to feed the marijuana plant, and they cryptococcus neoformans has been building up in it then spread to Joe and Foreman.

Cameron waits for the test results but the tests for cryptococcus neoformans are negative Joe goes into defib and Foreman tries to revive him without success.

## Words of the Day

Cryptococcus Neoformans: An encapsulated yeast-like fungus that can live in both plants and animals. It most often shows up in patients that are already immunocompromised, for instance by the AIDS virus.

## Memorable Quotes

House: Chase, stick your fingers in there (a patients brain's) and grope around until you find it. Wait, when you turn him into a vegetable there'll be frivolous lawsuits, you know what would be better? A contrast MRI, do we have one of those?
Dr. Chase: You can't do an MRI, if the bullet fragments are magnetic, they'll move around and rip his brains out.
House: Well, let's flip a coin, head: MRI, tails: he dies.

Dr. Foreman: Police-issue Kevlar vests don't have the ceramic plate insert that would shatter a bullet, they would just catch it. So the bullet shattered on its own, meaning Baby Shoes was using .38 calibre hollow points that, unfortunately, are ferromagnetic.
House: It's just so cool that you know that.

Police Officer Joe: (laughing) You have the right to remain...stupid!
Baby Shoes: Watch the gun.
Police Officer Joe: Anything you have to say will be completely incomprehensible... (still laughing hysterically)

Dr. Foreman: (My father) is not proud of me, he's proud of Jesus. Everything I do right is God's work, everything I do wrong is my own damn fault.

Dr. Chase: What are you looking for?
House: I called my mom, she didn't pick up.

Dr. Cameron: The chance of infection is next to nothing
House: Yeah, I was never that great at math, but next to nothing is higher than nothing, right?

Dr. Foreman: Drugs?
Dr. Chase: He's a cop.
Dr. Foreman: Good point. How about...drugs?

House: He did, however get hit by a bullet. Just mentioning...
Dr. Cameron: He was shot?
House: No – somebody threw it at him.

Dr. Cameron: Reliable witness?

House: His name's "Baby Shoes." How bad can he be?

Dr. Foreman: What's Dr. Cameron wearing?
Joe: Dark blue pants, white shirt, black shoes.
Dr. Foreman: Ooh, almost. Except for the pants, shirt, and shoes. You're blind.

House: I've got a disability.
Haines: These are speeding tickets.
House: Lot of emergencies.

House: Foreman, policeman are our friends. If you and I ever get separated shopping...
Dr. Cuddy: (to House) I can't even imagine the backward logic you used to rationalize shooting a corpse.
House: Well if I shot a live person there's a lot more paperwork.
Dr. Cuddy: Then it won't be a problem for you to stand beside a casket, and explain why a cancer patient has a bullet hole in his head.

Dr. Foreman: So I'm just a regular patient now?
House: No. You get your own thermometer.

Dr. Chase: You want to give Foreman a brain biopsy?
House: Come on, really, who doesn't?

House: Hey, I'm just messing with your head. Mother's maiden name?

Dr. Foreman: Get out of my temporal lobe, House.

# Euphoria (Part II)

This is the eighteenth episode of the second season of House.

## Synopsis

House goes to Cuddy to ask for a bone saw to get a brain sample of Joe's brain. Cuddy refuses, telling him she has called CDC. Foreman is not comforted since he knows he only has 36 hours. House goes to Foreman in quarantine and walks him through Joe's autopsy from outside the plastic tent. Cuddy calls in security but before they can get in, Foreman goes blind and is unable to get his sample.

House orders multiple treatments to cover all of his bases, in hopes that one will work, and goes to Joe's apartment. He is looking for the rat that Foreman had mentioned he saw the first time he was in the apartment. Foreman then calls his father while House watches the rat, waiting for it to manifest any symptoms.

While he waits, House meets with a clinic patient whose mother claims she's been having epileptic fits. House concludes that the girl is merely masturbating and has what he calls "gratification disorder."

Foreman recovers his sight but now they don't know which of all the prescribed treatments helped, and complicating things, his pancreas shut down from the treatments. House suggests they stop the treatment to buy time and Foreman agrees. Foreman's father arrives and House hustles him into Cuddy's office to explain the situation.

Rodney then talks his son, and Foreman lies to him about the fact that not only will he soon die, but he will die painfully. House is plotting how to get to Joe's corpse while Foreman and his mother who has Alzheimer's. Foreman is not terribly comforted when his father offers to pray for him.

Foreman's condition spirals downward, deteriorating even faster than Joe's did, and House notes that the rat captured from Joe's apartment still shows no symptoms. Cuddy goes to visit Foreman and he's furious she isn't letting the autopsy go ahead to save his life. House figures out that the cop had Legionnaire's disease, which slowed down the rate at which he was displaying symptoms. House exposes Foreman to it against his wishes.

Cameron monitors Foreman as his temperature drops. House wonders why the pain doesn't increase and why Cameron isn't getting sick. He concludes that Foreman's body isn't recognizing that he has the disease, and that the Legionnaire's triggered his antibodies. House thinks the answer is listeria but the treatment will kill the Legionnaire's as well. Foreman insists House do a white-matter biopsy on him, but House refuses.

House informs Foreman's father, Rodney, that they will soon have to put Foreman in a coma. Rodney agrees to let House take over the medical decisions his son will be incapable of making. Foreman suggests Cameron to act as his medical proxy and apologizes for stealing her article. Cameron refuses to accept his apology but agrees to act as his proxy. Her first task as his proxy is to press House to do the biopsy. She hassles him about it and he refuses.

Soon, Rodney becomes aware that Cameron, not him, is acting as his advocate as per his son's request, and is upset. House asks for one hour to go back to Joe's apartment and find a dead animal they can do a biopsy on, and if that doesn't work, he'll do the biopsy they are harassing him for. House goes to Joe's apartment without a hazmat suit and finds a blind pigeon concludes the water for Joe's marijuana is on a timed system. House figures out it's on a separate water system from the rest of the house and determines the culprit is the Naegleria parasite. He gives them the news but Cameron has already determined that from the biopsy she ordered when he was out of the hospital.

Cameron tells Rodney that Eric can be cured of the disease but they don't know how the biopsy affected him. When Foreman awakens, he discovers that he can't wiggle his left toes and when he tries to raise his right arm he raises his left arm instead.

## Words of the Day

Legionaire's: This is an infection caused by a bacteria. It can come in the form of an infection that precedes pneumonia, or can come as a milder respiratory illness.

Brain Biopsy: Brain biopsy is the removal of a small piece of brain tissue for the diagnosis of abnormalities of the brain.

## Memorable Quotes

Dr. Wilson: You haven't sprinkled granules on his donut? His bowels would open up like the red sea.
House: He wouldn't eat the donut.
Wilson: Have you seriously been down here for hours?
House: No. I had to pee a couple times.
Dr. Wilson: You've gotta stop blaming Cuddy for this.
House: Given that it is her fault, it's appropriate.
Dr. Wilson: That part is her fault. The part where somebody wasted his time in a basement plotting the overthrow of a government agency, that one's on you.

House: Forget it. You just biopsied a mattress.

Dr. Cuddy: (to House) Go to your office. Play with your ball. Write on your white board. Insult your team. Do whatever it is that you do to figure things out.

Dr. Cuddy: One afternoon, and you're on pace to set the record for most patients seen in a month!
House: You're upset that I'm doing clinic hours? Wow, that is so like rain on your wedding day.

Dr. Cameron: I'm trying to be professional, here. There's no need to be nasty.

Dr. Foreman: I'm in pain!
Dr. Cameron: So is House.
Dr. Foreman: And he's a delight!

Dr. Foreman: (to Cuddy) And the punishment for violating those regulations? Is it death? Because frankly, I'm okay if you get a fine, or suspension. Hell, you can spend a couple years in jail if it saves my life!

(House comes in with Foreman's father)
Cuddy: What is this?
House: He's not a what, he's a who. They even have the right to vote now.
Dr. Foreman: I'd rather be disabled than dead.
House: Sure, I make it look oh so sexy. It's actually not as glamorous as you might think.

House: First symptom is euphoria.
Dr. Wilson: How do you know if a rat's euphoric?
House: He doesn't usually climb on his water bottle like that, does he?

House: Cameron, what type of illnesses affect humans but not rats?
Dr. Cameron: Why are you asking me that?
House: Because I'm sure that you spent the first twelve years of your life dreaming of being a vet.

House: In actuality, all your little girl is doing...is saying "Yoo hoo to the who-who."
Claire: She's what?
House: "Marching the penguin." (Claire looks blank) "Ya-yaing the Sisterhood." "Finding Nemo." (Grace giggles) Liked that one.
Claire: Are you saying that my daughter (covers her daughter's ears) is masturbating?
House: I was trying to be discreet--there's a child in the room!
House: As soon as Steve the rat gets sick, I do an autopsy.
Dr. Wilson: As soon as he's dead.
House: Right after he gets sick, there's a good chance he'll get hit in the head with a...cane-shaped object.

Dr. Cameron: If it was toxic mold, I'd be sick.
House: How do we know you're not sick?
Dr. Cameron: Do I seem happy to you?
House: Never.

Dr. Cuddy: A thin slice of Joe's brain could also cause a public health crisis.
House: It's not a good idea to scream "Fire" every time someone lights a match.

Dr. Foreman: I'm okay?

House: Your breath stinks and you're peeing into a bag. What are our names?

Dr. Foreman: You did the biopsy? Thank you.

House: Names.

Dr. Foreman: Cameron, my dad, and the manipulative bastard.

House: You remembered.

House: I screwed up.

Dr. Cameron: How can you not capture a blind bird?

House: That's not what I meant. I screwed up the first time through this place.

Dr. Wilson: Why weren't you with Foreman?

House: I hang out in the basement, you rag on me. I stay in my office, you rag on me. Honky just can't buy a break.

House: That was great!

Dr. Cameron: It was rude and unnecessary.

House: Yeah!

House: Pain makes us make bad decisions, fear of pain is almost as big a motivator.

Rodney: My son says you're a manipulative bastard.

House: It's a pet name. I call him "Dr. Bling."

Dr. Cameron: Foreman's black.
House: What? How long have you been sitting on this information?

House: Philosophical question – how do you want to die?
Dr. Foreman: Old age.

Rose: You're a goof.
House: Takes one to know one, loser. Wait, that means I'm a loser – scratch that.

Dr. Wilson: You're accessing a web cam?
House: Cuddy's shower. Are you a fan of the Brazilian?

# Forever

This is the nineteenth episode of the second season of House, MD

## Synopsis

A young father named Brent wakes up in the morning when he hears the baby crying. He manages to wake himself up and get ready for work. Meanwhile, his young wife Kara appears with the baby, who has colic, and says she is going to give him a bath. He is almost out the door for work but vomits halfway up the stairs and returns. He comes back up to the bathroom to find his wife in the bathtub with the baby. She has passed out, and the baby is under water.

Kara and her baby Mikey are taken by EMTs to the clinic where Chase is the attending physician. Foreman soon arrives, still recovering from his biopsy, and House is skeptical. House is not impressed with Kara's seizure symptoms and he and his team eliminate the obvious causes one by one.

House sneaks into Cuddy's office to meet her when she comes in and they spar over her "date" with Wilson—in reality they are going out to dinner to discuss funding for the clinic. As he teases her about this alleged business dinner, the baby's lung collapses while Kara has another seizure in the MRI.

Mother and child have recovered for now House picks up on Foreman's suggested diagnosis: myelomas meningitis. Chase is skeptical of House's distrust for patients but House reminds him of the drug-dealing cop that almost killed Foreman. House tells Chase to give the baby ECMO treatment to remove and recycle his blood.

House, after going through Cuddy's garbage, shows Wilson that he found a bottle of Red Clover - which leads House to suspect that she cancer and she wants Wilson for a consult. He is interrupted when Cameron tells him that Kara's blood isn't clotting and she is also an alcoholic. When Foreman doesn't argue with House's prescribed treatment—to induce a coma before she gets the DTs-- House orders Foreman to argue with him as he used to do.

Wilson and Cuddy go on their dinner date and they have an awkward chat over Wilson's divorce and don't manage to get to business concerns. Kara wakes up and Foreman learns that Brent and Kara met in AA. House and Foreman are discussing the case when House notices the baby is missing. It turns out that Kara is trying to smother him.

Brent won't accept that Kara tried to kill their son. Cameron thinks that Kara may be psychotic and that she faked a seizure when her husband caught her trying to kill Mikey, but House believes otherwise. While Cameron expresses her own frustration with Foreman over his complacency and tranquil attitude, Wilson administers a cancer test to a spoon he took from his dinner with Cuddy. He wants to see if the Red Clover really does mean she thinks she has cancer.

Mikey's heart rate is increasing while Kara's brainwaves indicate that she has another situation. Her body, however, she doesn't react and they conclude she's in encephalopathic delirium as a result of vitamin deficiency. The baby, unable to handle the stress of being drowned and smothered all in one day, dies.

Kara awakens and suddenly memories flood in—she realizes what she did to her son. Foreman finally tells her that Mikey died and she starts crying before she vomits blood. They try to diagnose her new symptoms while Chase tries wrestles with his guilt over prescribing the wrong treatment for Mikey. House finds Brent holding his dead son, and requests the baby's body for a biopsy. Unafraid to kick a man while he's down, House gets Brent to admit his was drunk the morning that his son almost drowned, and for many months had avoided facing up to Kara's psychosis.

Chase, moved by the spirit, says a prayer over Mikey's body before doing the autopsy. Cuddy's spoon tested negative for cancer, and meanwhile, Chase discovers the baby's intestines showed flattened vili. House concludes that both the baby and mother had celiac disease, which is triggered by stress. The disease damaged their small intestines, which led to vitamin deficiency. Chase's treatment didn't work because this damage prevented the baby absorbing the medicine, and led to Kara getting stomach cancer.

House then meets with Cuddy and after needling her about her estrogen levels and her garbage, gets her to admit that she's taking fertility meds with Red Clover as an herbal booster. Cuddy's trying to get pregnant and is looking for a donor, and wanted to keep it secret.

Kara refuses to let anyone treat her and House talks to her. She doesn't want to live and House accepts that.

Brent goes in to see Kara and asks her to ask Mikey for forgiveness for him when she meets him, presumably in heaven. House doesn't reveal to Wilson what Cuddy was up to. Foreman works to master his knowledge of medical terminology again.

## Words of the Day

Coeliac Disease: This is an autoimmune disorder of the small intestine. Coeliac disease is caused by a reaction to a certain gluten protein found in wheat . Upon exposure, the enzyme tissue of he bowel modifies the protein, and the immune system cross-reacts with the bowel tissue, causing an inflammatory reaction. That leads to the flattening of the small intestine, and reduced ability to absorb nutrients.

## Memorable Quotes

House: (to Chase) So why are you down here? Hoping to expand your make-out pool to include the preemie to nine-year old demographic?

Dr. Chase: EGMO could kill him!
House: You don't start him on EGMO and that infection can rampage through his body like Pistons fans after a championship.

House: I don't care how guilty you feel or how touched you are by his reborn spirit...
Dr. Cameron: I'm not touched.
House: Then you're guilt-ridden
Dr. Cameron: I'm not guilt-ridden!
House: Then you're pathetic!
Dr. Cameron: Right now I'm annoyed!

House: Bad news: estrogen is too high.
Dr. Cuddy: No matter how many people you tell otherwise, I am, and always have been, a woman. Estrogen is normal.

Dr. Wilson: I'm checking her saliva for cancer markers.
House: Yeah... I do that after all my dates...

House: She's my boss. If she gets sick the hospital might want to replace her. Especially if she dies. I'll have to learn how to manipulate someone new.

Dr. Cameron: He got sick doing his job.
House: Well if he got killed doing his job I wouldn't keep him on the payroll.

Dr. Foreman: You're addicted to conflict.
House: (taking a Vicodin) Did they change the name?

House: What, don't you want to work for me? I'm nice, I'm fun at parties...

House: What you've got there? Special panties for your date with Wilson?
Dr. Cuddy: It's not a date. And it's none of your business.
House: If it's not a date it is business, and if it was business you wouldn't say it was none of my business.
Dr. Cuddy: What do you want?
House: I want to talk about your date with Wilson.
Dr. Cuddy: It's not a date.
House: This is fun.

House: So, what causes seizures, hypercalcemia, and the thing where Mommy bends like Gumby?
House: I take it black. Like I take my brain-damaged neurologists.

House: Well done. But until you can remember how to make coffee...hands off the patients.

House: What's that saying? When you assume you become an ass to me.

House: Tonight – "L" Word marathon.
Dr. Wilson: You watch The "L" Word?
House: On mute.

House: I ask you, is almost dying any excuse for not being fun?
House: Idiots are fun – no wonder every village wants one.

House: Hey, take it easy on Foreman – he's playing with one lobe tied behind his back.

House: The thing about being a good loser--it means you're still a loser.

House: Ideas are not soda cans. Recycling sucks. Give me something new and shiny.

House: You don't have cancer.
Dr. Cuddy: You don't have dwarfism.
House: You have no proof of that.

Kara: I killed my son.
House: Is it my turn to say something obvious now?

# Who's Your Daddy?

This is the twentieth episode of the second season of House, MD.

## Synopsis

Leona and her father Crandall are taking a plane and talking about the fact that she lost her mother. Also they are talking about how she survived eight months after Katrina on her own and found out Crandall is her father. Then she starts to hallucinate that the plane is flooding, and collapses.

House is experiencing a bout of insomnia , and when he comes in to the hospital in the morning, he is sleepy, irritable, and in pain. He's about to take morphine when Cuddy calls with Leona's case. When she collapses, she went into cardiac shock but didn't have a heart attack. Her father immediately recognizes House as an old friend and is thrilled that the he is the one on his daughter's case. House, however, is openly skeptical about this newfound daughter, smelling a scam.

House treats the girl nonetheless, suspecting arrhythmia. He decides to induce it to eventually pinpoint the part of the heart causing the hallucinations and administer treatment.

House goes to Cuddy after reviewing her choice of sperm donors and expresses disgust over all of them, trying to convince her that getting a sperm donor is a horrible idea.

Meanwhile, Leona isn't doing so well. Leona hallucinates that her dead mother in the next bed, dripping wet. House wonders if Leona's visions are in response to pain. There is only one-way to test it: to hurt her. House pricks her with a pin and simultaneously accuses her of scamming his friend. She starts to cry but eventually hallucinates in response to the pain.

House is still having trouble with his leg and determines that Leona's problems are due to auto-immune deficiency. Crandall demands that House use his bone marrow for a transplant. He also refuses to let House do a paternity test because he feels that this will show Leona he doesn't trust her.

House meets with a mother and her child whose skin is turning red, and House quickly informs her that he has been sitting on a red couch. He's interrupted by Cuddy who needs him to give her a fertility injection. He injects her in the ass and tells her that this is a dumb idea.

Leona is hooked up for more tests when a thick black substance oozes from Leona's mouth. They determine it contains stool samples—it's essentially supposed to be coming out the other end. It turns out that there's a blockage in her digestive system and it's working in reverse. They start a liver biopsy and House advises Crandall not to get attached to her, confessing that he once slept with Crandall's fiancée. This does little to convince him to take the paternity test.

Leona is getting her liver biopsy when House halts it. He had listened to a CD of her grandfather, a famous jazz musician who was having trouble making out pitch that was actually correct. House also determines she has iron deposits in her melanin like her grandfather.

House then meets with a new intern, Patrick, in Cuddy's office. He is completely socially inept, and she soon figures out that Patrick is one of her potential donors and scrams. Chase gives Leona the treatment House recommended but the iron damages her lungs and she goes into respiratory distress. House figures since the iron is supposed to be discharged as waste but Leona's waste system isn't working, the iron went to her lungs and attached to mold picked up in the aftermath of Katrina.

House gives Cuddy her next injection and suggests she finds someone she knows, likes, and trusts to give her sperm. Cameron soon appears up to break the news that Leona's treatment isn't working. It's back to diagnostic and House determines Leona was lying about where she may have picked up the mold, so he goes to wake her up and question her. She finally admits she was lying and writes down where she was.

House reveals to the staff that Leona was at a recording studio in New Orleans, and they try to figure out which mold she has in her lungs. Leona starts to revive and House tells her he conducted a paternity test without Crandall's permission and Crandall is her father. But later at his apartment he reads the paternity test, which confirms Leona isn't Crandall's daughter. He doesn't tell Crandall the truth.

## Words of the Day

Sperm Donor: A man who gives or sells his semen to be used specifically to produce a baby. The cost of donor sperm in the United States ranges from around $200 -

$3,000 per vial unit of semen, usually a quantity of around 0.7 ml. Donors give their sperm by reaching orgasm at clinics called sperm banks. They have to pass a test to make sure they have a clean medical history and are not predisposed to any diseases.

## Memorable Quotes

House: Here is how to become a great artist: First, get miserable. Misery drives you to become a great artist, but the art does nothing for your misery, which drives you to drugs, which makes you a lousy artist!

Dr. Wilson: I find it very comforting, you defending a man you haven't seen in years--to know my friend, no matter what, will always be my champion, my protector.
House: I'm not protecting him, I'm smacking her.
Dr. Wilson: The modesty of a true hero!
House: Push me and I'll let her die, just so you'll stop annoying me.

House: How does somebody who believes absolutely anything become a non-fiction writer?

Crandall: And I'm her father.

House: Hmm. Yeah, she looks just like you. Got the same ' fro.

Crandall: I wrote a book about Baker. Hung out with him. And his daughter.

House: That is how babies are made.

Dr. Cuddy: The guy who brought the girl in, says he knows you. I thought I knew all your friend.

House: Do I know you?

Crandall: C'mon, it's me, Crandall.

House: Doesn't ring a bell.

Crandall: I can't believe...

House: Unless you mean Dylan Crandall, the man who'll believe anything. Because I just made you believe...

Dr. Cameron: I can handle a simple consent form.

House: Okay, I'll be Crandall. "Dr. Cameron..."

Dr. Foreman: House, from what you say this guy will trust you...

House: Are you in this scene? Go.

Dr. Cameron: I need to talk to you about a procedure we'd like to do on Leona.

House: "Like to do"? Is this fun for you?

Dr. Cameron: He's not you—he's not going to mock me.

House: Stay in character. "I'm so scared—hold me."

House: Donor 1284 likes square dancing. No one likes square dancing.

Dr. Cuddy: You didn't tell anyone else what I'm doing?
House: Not a soul.
Dr. Cuddy: Wilson? Cameron? Maybe you mentioned it to her.
House: No, I'm really a good secret-keeper. Never told anyone that Wilson wets his bed. Oh, you tricked me.

Dr. Wilson: You didn't run the test?
House: Said I wouldn't.
Dr. Wilson: Okay, so either you lied, or he has pictures of you being nice.

Dr. Cameron: She's a Katrina victim.
House: She's better than Crandall – he's a Katrina victim's victim.

House: Pretentiousness is hereditary. Just because they haven't found the gene yet...

Crandall: If our friendship means anything to you...
House: Do you know anything about me at all?

House: Don't try to talk. You've got a big medical thing in your mouth.

House: That black ooze we saw - that was a bowel movement. Out of her mouth.
Wilson: You're trying to end this conversation by grossing me out? I'm an oncologist. Half my patients have their skin sloughing off.

House: So, what is she, Foreman? A light-skinned black chick or dark-skinned white chick?

Crandall: Heard about your leg.
House: Yeah, pulled my hamstring playing Twister. Just gonna walk it off.

House: You've reached a number that has been disconnected and is no longer in service. If you feel you have reached this recording in error, go with it, hang up, on three. One, two...*beep*
Cuddy: House, pick up. I know it's your day off. And you've no doubt got lots of exciting plans, but I've got a case.

Cuddy: Need you. Now.
House: Yes, Mistress.

Chase: Her heart's fragile after that last attack! The chances of tachycardia are...

House: You have my permission to blame Foreman in any negligence trial.

## No Reason

This is the final episode of the second season of House.

## Synopsis

A man named Vince, suffering from an extremely swollen tongue and a temperature of 103, is admitted and assigned to House. Foreman is about to leave for the day when a man comes in, identifies House, and shoots him twice.,

House wakes up two days later to find Cameron at his bedside and learns that the shooter was caught—he was shot by a security guard when he left. House staggers out to visit Vince, still interested in the case, but Cameron tells him to focus on getting better. House then goes to Cuddy and reveals that his leg pain feels better, even without the morphine. House assumes something went wrong with the surgery.

House then seeks out the shooter to ask why he did what he did The man says he wanted House to live and suffer. House calmly responds in kind, turning off the man's morphine drip.

Foreman and Chase are doing a biopsy on Vince which triggers a seizure, and the staff go to House for input. House tells them to do a lumbar puncture despite protests from Foreman as to the risks.

That night the shooter reveals House treated his wife, who lived. House's care of his wife was not the issue. He shot House because during his wife's stay at the hospital, he told House he'd had an affair. The affair had nothing to do with his wife's sickness but House told her anyway, and she committed suicide.

House goes out and checks in on Vince and meets his wife Judy. She is stunning, and her husband is quite plain. Struggling to understand what would drive her to marry a man who isn't as good looking as her, he asks a rather personal question—has she had an affair? She tells him she's always been faithful. Vince's lumbar puncture goes well at first, but when it's over his eye fills with blood and pops out due to the pressure.

At the same time House starts bleeding after he tears out his stitches. They put House back together and he argues with the shooter over his affair and gets more details—his wife killed herself in the garage of the home they shared. House then orders some tests, and when he mentions the wife Judy, Cameron reveals Vince is a widower.

House is talking with Wilson and wonders if "Judy" was a hallucination that House has conjured in order to cope with being shot. House still is worried if he is hallucinating because the surgery caused neural damage. He then asks Cuddy why a surgeon administered ketamine and put him in a disassociative coma. Cuddy says she ordered the treatment as a chance to give House his leg again, but he's upset that she did so without his permission and approval.

Meanwhile, Vince's tests give no useful information. The shooter challenges House on Chase's diagnosis, taunting him and noting that House might be getting dumber. Vince is back out of post-op but the recent surgery didn't help and he soon starts bleeding from the groin.

House considers the new symptom and first suggests kidney issues, and when Foreman suggests something far more plausible- testicular cancer--House is worried that he has brain damage because he missed that. Wilson suggests House doesn't want the pain in his leg to cease because wants a reason to be unhappy, and defends Cuddy for trying to help him, even without this permission. House wonders why Wilson is defending Cuddy and figures out Wilson knew about Cuddy's plan as well. He hits Wilson and then he realizes he hallucinated the whole thing, he's back in his bed, and the shooter taunts him.

House tries out his new leg and then wonders how he got to his meeting – he doesn't remember how he got from the ICU to the hallway. House then goes to Cuddy and takes himself off the case, admitting he's blacking out. Cuddy however confirms House's previous "hallucination" was actually real, and determines that now he's actually hallucinating. He's again back in his bed, as the shooter looks on.

House has lunch with the shooter at the taco place and wonders what is and isn't a hallucination, although he's pretty sure that he wouldn't' be having lunch with the man who tried to shoot him—he now must be hallucinating for sure. The shooter suggests he just keeps tossing out suggestions as to Vince's treatment and his team will correct him if he's wrong.

House, hallucination or not, thinks this is good advice. He questions the basics of the biopsy and suggests they do surgery but Chase believes that the risks are too great. House comes up with a way to do the surgery using a robot and House tells Vince he has no choice.

House is back in bed going over the tests and the shooter taunts him over the lack of meaning in his life. House hallucinates again. This time, he thinks he's in a car with

Judy as she committed suicide, then turns with a tear in his eye and apologizes.

House goes into the surgery room and points out the staff never pulled him off the case, and never challenged him on any of his theories, and then tries to stop the surgery. He thinks he needs to push the hallucination to its limits and tries to operate on Vince, cutting into him and killing him. A bullet falls out of Vince's hand. House picks it up then wakes up to realize he's being rushed to the E.R. moments after being shot. House tells them to tell Cuddy to administer the ketamine.

## INDEX

www.ingramcontent.com/pod-product-compliance
Lightning Source LLC
Chambersburg PA
CBHW022016090426
42739CB00006BA/157
* 9 7 8 1 6 0 3 3 2 0 6 5 8 *